HISTORY IN ART

HISTORY IN ART

by
Ariane Ruskin

FRANKLIN WATTS, INC.
NEW YORK 1974

The author wishes to thank the following for permission to quote briefly: Bernard Berenson, *The Italian Painters of the Renaissance*, by permission of The Clarendon Press, Oxford; *Larousse Encyclopedia of Modern History*, edited by Marcel Dunan and John Roberts, reproduced by permission of The Hamlyn Publishing Group Limited; Helène Nolthenius, *In That Dawn*, by permission of Darton, Longman and Todd, Ltd.; and Zoë Oldenbourg, *The Crusades*, translated by Anne Carter, © 1966 by Random House, Inc., by permission of Pantheon Books/A Division of Random House.

PHOTOGRAPHS COURTESY OF George Rainbird Ltd. with the exception of the following; Charles Phelps Cushing, New York City, page 178; The Louvre Museum, Paris, page 18; The Museum of Modern Art, New York City, pages 287 and 294; Scala New York/Florence, pages 6 and 16; Trustees of the British Museum, London, page 15; and University of Virginia Library, Charlottesville, Virginia, page 207.

Library of Congress Cataloging in Publication Data

Ruskin, Ariane.
    History in art.

    Bibliography: p.
    1. Art–History. 2. History in art.
N5303.R87   709   73–5673
ISBN 0-531-01988-8

CONTENTS

LIST OF
ILLUSTRATIONS

I

Greece and Rome

II

The Art of the Middle Ages

III

The Renaissance

IV

Spain and the Netherlands

V

France and England

VI

The Nineteenth Century

VII

The Modern World

1. Bison: from the Lascaux Caves, about 12,000 B.C. Dordogne, France. *Photo courtesy of Life Magazine, Time-Life, Inc.*

INTRODUCTION

BECAUSE OF the camera, the world of today is always before our eyes. There is hardly a political figure or person of importance in the arts or science whose face is not familiar to us — who is not to be seen in a wide assortment of magazines and newspapers or in films. Nor is there a corner of the earth whose landscape would be strange to us. In a way, then, it is hard for us to imagine that this was not always so. But photography is a new phenomenon. As recently as the past century, and for all the millennia before, men could know only the faces of the people they had actually met and only the scenery of cities and countries they had actually visited — a narrow slice of the world, considering the limitations of travel until very recently. To know more than this, they were obliged to turn to the artist.

From very earliest times (Plate 1) the artist was always there, carefully depicting and recording the world he saw around him, and always in a way he felt would not only convey the appearance of things but also give pleasure to the beholder. This need to create art, or rather to re-create the visual world by means of inanimate materials — using stone to replace flesh or colors on a flat surface to re-create three-dimensional scenes — seems always to have existed in man. Even thirty thousand years ago the men of the Old Stone Age in Europe covered the walls of their caves with vivid, lifelike paintings of the animals they hunted. To create these paintings, they used many pigments, or coloring substances, carefully prepared and applied with brushes of split wood or fur. They also sculpted their models with fully rounded realism. Moreover, the artist of the Old Stone Age was a student who studied with a master, perhaps for years, before he was allowed to create works of his own — and this at a time when man dressed in animal furs, when he did not know how to build a house or use a wheel or grow the simplest crop. It was the artist, then, who for millennia, even when the written word did not exist, "held the mirror up to nature."

Since the days of ancient Egypt, the artist has mirrored the manner of man's dress, his architecture, and the occupations with which he has busied himself — in short, the entire visual world with which he was familiar. Plate 2 is a copy of a fresco from the tomb of Nakht, an Egyptian of about 1500 B.C. We see here, in all probability, two views of Nakht, accompanied by his wife and children, busy at a favorite Egyptian sport — hunting for fowl in the marshes of the Nile. If we look at the picture carefully, it will tell us much. We can see how the hunting of birds was conducted with throwing sticks, and what fish lived in the water beneath the hunters' feet, and what birds roosted in the swamp and flew in the air above, all carefully drawn to the last detail. The repeated pattern of parallel lines between water and sky represents thickly growing papyrus plants with their bell-shaped flowers. The skiffs in which the figures stand are made of these hollow papyrus stalks lashed together. The picture tells us, too, how the Egyptians would have looked if we had met them: the men dressed only in elaborately folded kilts, and the women in tight sheaths extending from breast level to the floor. The cloth of both these garments was a white linen, which could be transparently sheer; color was provided by heavy necklaces, bracelets, and headbands of brightly colored beads. The women were slender, the men broad-shouldered (this must have been the Egyptian ideal), and both wore heavy black wigs, although of different styles. These fashions changed only once in the three-thousand-year history of ancient Egyptian art, which gives us some idea of the changelessness of Egyptian society.

In other paintings from the walls of tombs we see men at work (Plate 3), women in bright cosmetics and diaphanous dresses at a party, dancers and musicians — every detail, in fact, of Egyptian life. Historic events,

2. *Fowling in the Marshes.* Copy of fresco from the tomb of Nakht, about 1500 B.C. *London, British Museum.*

too, are depicted, not only on the walls of tombs, but on boxes, chairs, tables, and every sort of household object. And these are not only painted but also worked in gold, silver, and precious stones. Moreover, the rulers of Egypt are portrayed again and again. Their colossal statues, chiseled in the hardest stones, appear in their tombs, personal temples, and the temples built to their gods. The Egyptians possessed an easy, cursive script,

3. Egyptian mural — men feeding oryxes, about 1500 B.C. *London, British Museum.*

but if they had written not a word, we would still have a clear vision of their industrious life and balmy pleasures, and some idea of their history.

And so the artist gives us a cameraman's view of every period in history, but as we shall see, he also does a great deal more, and cameralike realism is often far from his mind.

The artist of the Old Stone Age painted only animals. In his art, little stick figures of men appear but rarely, and there is no trace of any landscape whatever. Moreover, these animals were man's prey. Curiously, too, the paintings appear not in the caves in which the people spent their daily lives, but in tiny caverns sometimes as much as a mile below the surface, where there is no trace of habitation. All this tells the trained anthropologist something that might not be immediately evident to us: these paintings had a magical purpose; the artist hoped, by painting an animal in the most realistic way possible, to gain power over that animal in the chase. In fact, the animals are often shown pierced with weapons, and sometimes the paintings themselves have been battered with sharp instruments.

Curiously enough, the many paintings that cover the walls of Egyptian tombs were created in this same spirit of "sympathetic magic." The Egyptian attitude toward death was one we might find difficult to understand: the people of ancient Egypt fought death in the very burial mound itself. They believed that if the flesh of the deceased could be preserved by mummification, he would not truly die, but would only go to the "Court of Re across the Lily Lake." But the dead man would need food in the next world — enough of it to last him throughout eternity. He would need clothing, too, and servants, pets, furniture, games, cosmetics — everything he needed in this world. If he were a child, he would need toys. As many of these objects were placed in the tomb as possible, and those that could not be left were represented on the walls of the tombs and tomb chapels, where the dead man was depicted at every pastime he enjoyed in life and which it was hoped he would continue to enjoy after death. His servants were portrayed, too, busily tending his crops, preparing his food, rowing boats, milling flour, making jewelry, and following every conceivable occupation to fill their master's needs. It was hoped that they would continue to work for their master forever. At first, only kings could enjoy such elaborate burials, but later these burials were available to any man who could afford to build a tomb (typically a square "mastaba," with slanting sides and a flat roof) and hire an artist.

We may notice that the figures in the tomb paintings are represented in an unusual way, with the head and legs in profile while the eyes and shoulders are viewed from the front (Plate 4). It may be agreed that it is easier to paint the human figure in such a way, but this technique seems also to have served a magical purpose: all the parts of such a figure are portrayed — both arms, both legs, front and back, as well as a complete eye. Thus the entire figure would survive eternally, and not just those parts that happened to be visible at any given moment.

So passionate was the desire of the Egyptians to deny death, and to preserve for the dead person the life he knew well, that they re-created in the finest detail their world of secure plenty and superb elegance (Plate 5). And so, while they may not have succeeded in giving immortality to

4. Egyptian mural (detail): from a tomb at Thebes, about 1500 B.C. *London, British Museum.*

5. Egyptian mural — guests, dancing girls, and musicians: from a tomb at Thebes, about 1500 B.C. *London, British Museum.*

6. Statue in diorite of King Chephren of the Fourth
Dynasty, about 2700 B.C. *Cairo, U.A.R., Cairo Museum.*

the deceased, the artists of ancient Egypt managed to do something they could not have expected to do: they gave immortality to their own golden way of life, about which, were it not for their efforts, we would know very little indeed.

The Egyptians were splendid portraitists. Egyptian art shows us many faces and types — fat and flabby noblemen, humpbacked dwarfs, dark-eyed and full-lipped women — which must have been telling likenesses of their models. And yet, when we look at the statues of the kings, they appear suspiciously alike. Moreover, this similarity seems to have been deliberate. Kings are known to have usurped the statues of earlier rulers simply by changing the name on the base. In fact, many Egyptian statues, especially those of rulers, are "idealized." By this we mean that they resembled not the individual they were meant to represent, but an ideal type of what a king *should* look like. So King Chephren of the Fourth Dynasty (a dynasty is a family of rulers) may well have been short and fat with a double chin and a wart on his nose, but he has been depicted for eternity as broad-shouldered and narrow-waisted, with a face of impassive grandeur — an expressionless ideal of serene majesty (Plate 6).

So it is that the artist tells us not only how man and his world looked in every age, but also how he wanted to look, what his aspirations, his greatest loves, and deepest religious beliefs were. In short, in every period the artist has reflected in his work not only nature but also man's very soul.

I

GREECE and ROME

VIRTUALLY ALL THE peoples of the world have their art, and their character and history are reflected in that art, but we will speak of only the history of what we call the Western world, of Europe and America. The art of the Western world had its beginning, with much of the rest of the culture of the West, in Greece.

The archaeologists who have dug among the ruins of the cities and towns of ancient Greece have found no palaces. The homes of the Greeks, whether peasants or rulers, were modest. Although they have long since disappeared, we do know that they contained no works of art. The splendid buildings that have been found, the world-famous examples of Greek architecture, were temples, *stoa* (roofed marketplaces), theaters, and such created not for individuals but for the various city-states of Greece. These buildings were made of stone, often of the finest marble, and it is in them, and more especially in the temples, that the great works of art have been found. Greek art, then, was created for the state and not for individual men.

This should not surprise us. From earliest times, "good laws" were the great interest of the Greeks. During the fifth century B.C. — the Golden Age — the men of Athens went to the assemblies, where all qualified citizens (and this did not include women and slaves) were free to speak and vote on every law, and any citizen might hold office by drawing lots. How could men best be ruled? This was the question that haunted their greatest thinkers. Some, like Plato, were not sure that a democracy such as that of Athens was ideal. In his *Republic*, he proposed one of the most intriguing of all answers to that question. Government was the passionate interest of every Greek citizen, and we can understand why their other great love, art, was devoted to the glorification of the state.

When we speak of the Golden Age of Greece, we find that we are speaking of Athens. There, art was shaped directly by history. In 480 B.C., the Persian King Xerxes descended on Greece with an army that may have been five million in number. Greece was divided into many city-states, and it was the city of Athens, along with Sparta, that heroically gathered together the tiny army of defenders, twenty thousand strong, and repelled the "barbarians," as the Greeks called their enemy. The sacred buildings of the Acropolis of Athens were destroyed by the invader, but her wise ruler, Themistocles, had prepared a navy to meet the threat. It was he who tricked the enemy into entering the Bay of Salamis where the Athenians destroyed Xerxes's fleet. Thus the greatest power among the old civilizations of the East was driven out of Europe forever. Some scholars feel that this was the moment of the very birth of Western culture.

When the Persians retreated, the Greek city-states formed the Delian League, with its headquarters on the island of Delos, to counter future invasions. Athens was, naturally, at the head of the league and she bore the burden of defense. At this point the Athenians, under the leadership of Pericles, did something that may shock us, even at this distance in time. They "appropriated" the funds of the Delian League, meant for defense, and used them to reconstruct the buildings of their Acropolis. Athens was meant to provide defense, and defense she would provide, as Pericles argued in the *Lives of Plutarch*:

"Not a horse do they furnish, not a ship, not a hoplite, but money simply, and this belongs not to those who give it, but to those who take it. . . . And it is but meet that the city, when once she is sufficiently equipped to prosecute the war, should apply her abundance to such works as, by their completion, will bring her everlasting glory. . . ."

Everlasting glory was certainly achieved. Under the general direction of Phidias, the greatest sculptor of the century, the richly decorated temples on the Acropolis rose to be among the supreme architectural and artistic achievements of all time. So it was that if art glorified the Greek state, the state devoted its greatest resources to art. And as in art, Athens took the lead in philosophy, drama, and all forms of culture except, ironically, the waging of war.

Above all, Greek artists concentrated on portraying the human form. Athletics and the development of the body fascinated the Greeks from the earliest times. Their Olympic Games date back to the dark age of 776 B.C., only a century after the *Iliad* was written, during the archaic period when what we now call Greek culture had its very beginnings. These games, athletic competitions of all sorts, were among the few things that united all Greeks. They were of such importance that all events were dated by Olympiads, four-year periods beginning with each new set of games. The statues of this dark age were often of nude males. These *kouroi* (a Greek word meaning "youths") sometimes represented gods such as Apollo and sometimes winners in the games. To the Greeks, the athlete with every muscle perfectly developed was the closest model they could find on earth for the eternal gods of Olympus.

Let us look at such a *kouros* (Plate 1). He seems stiff, frontal, and incapable of motion. His shoulders seem too broad, his hips too narrow, his head too large, and the features of his face do not seem to grow from the flesh, nor does his hair look like anything but an unnatural wig. Still this is a powerful figure, and we feel that here is a man to be reckoned with.

But the Greeks were striving, searching for a truer representation of man himself. And the defeat of the Persians, a century after this figure was

1. Greek *kouros* (youth), archaic. *Athens, National Museum.*

2. Myron. *Discobolus* (Roman copy), 460–450 B.C. *Rome, Museo Nazionale Romano.*

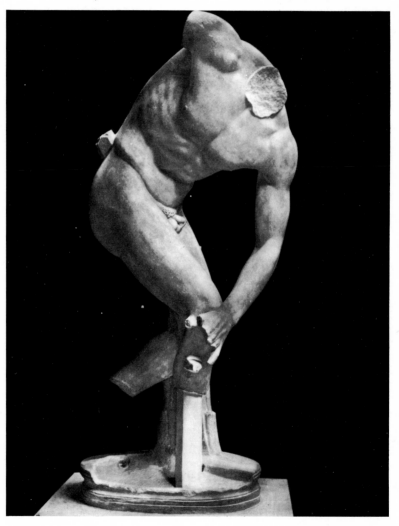

carved, ushered in a period of extraordinary revolution in the arts. The Greeks seem to have felt that if they could conquer Xerxes and his armies, they could overcome any challenge. It was a period of great pride and daring in Athens, and within the space of no more than a few years her sculp-

4. Polycleitos. *Doryphorus* (Roman copy),
about 450 B.C. *Naples, Italy, Museo Nazionale.*

3. Polycleitos. *Diadoumenos* (Roman copy), about 440 B.C. *Athens, National
Museum* (left).

tors discovered how to portray the human figure with a realism achieved
rarely again and a grace never surpassed. Perhaps the first artist of this revolution was Myron (fifth century B.C.), sculptor of the *Discobolus*, or *The
Discus Thrower* (Plate 2). Here we see that the body suddenly moves
freely and all the muscles are understood and in their proper places, although the surface of the flesh still appears hard. Polycleitos's two great
figures, the *Diadoumenos*, or *The Head Hunter* (Plate 3), and the *Doryphorus*, or *The Staff Bearer* (Plate 4), are softer and more relaxed. They
shift their weight from one leg to the other in a position of easy motion
we find often in Greek sculpture. But greatest of all were the works of
Phidias, every one of which has been lost. We can tell, though, from the
statuary of the Parthenon (the Temple of Athena), the building of which
he oversaw, what they must have been like — forms of physical perfection,
the women draped in diaphanous and billowing cloth through which their
soft flesh can be seen (Plate 5). All Greek sculpture was painted (a fact

which may surprise us), and so the forms originally presented an even greater effect of life than the cold white marble we see today.

These figures strike us immediately as somewhat strange. They are not people we would expect to meet on the street; they are too perfect. Like the Egyptian pharaohs, they are idealized, although they often represent not gods or rulers, but individual athletes. In fact, Greek artists of the fifth century idealized all their figures, human and divine, and this idealization was very much a part of their philosophy. Socrates and his follower Plato taught that there existed in eternity an *eidos*, a perfect form of all things we see on earth — a perfect circle, for example, which all circles created by the hand of man must resemble. So there was a perfect state with per-

5. *Diana and Aphrodite:* from east pediment of the Parthenon, Athens, 437–432 B.C. *London, British Museum.*

fect laws and a perfect man in mind and body. It was this perfection that the artists of Athens sought.

But the Greeks of the fifth century also admired portraits. There seems to have been, in fact, a portrait gallery on the Acropolis. We might well suppose, then, that there were busts of recognizable humans with all their individual faults. But the portraits, too, were idealized. One, a head of Pericles of which we have a copy (Plate 6), shows not the man as he must have looked, but a ruler as distinguished and ideal as Pharaoh. The best-loved work in the gallery was a portrait of Alcibiades, Socrates's favorite pupil, the most brilliant of all Athenian generals — one moment the darling of the public and the next in disgrace. Alcibiades was also considered

6. Portrait bust of Pericles. *Rome, Vatican Museum.*

the handsomest man in Athens, the closest to ideal perfection, and so his portrait may well have been a true likeness, not because it resembled a real man, but because Alcibiades resembled a god.

The Battle of Salamis is recorded nowhere in Greek art. The Greeks of the fifth century B.C. were not interested in the fleeting present but in the eternal, and so they depicted scenes from their mythology. This mythology was an inspiration for all the arts — poetry, drama, and literature, as well as sculpture and painting. It consisted of deeply moving stories explaining the seeming miracles of nature — the rising and setting of the sun, the changes of the seasons. The all-powerful gods of Olympus — the family of Zeus — around whom the stories were spun, were very like the gods of other neighboring religions, but in Greece they were envisioned by a race of poets. Hera, the jealous wife; Athena, the goddess of wisdom and the brave protectress of Athens, with her curls pushed under her helmet; Aphrodite, the gentle and sometimes wrathful goddess of love, married to the deformed Hephaestus, blacksmith to the gods — all these have such human qualities that they have never lost their appeal to the imagination. And in the great cycles of Greek mythology we also find vague memories of Greek history from the distant past, from the times before the dark age that stretched from the tenth to the seventh century B.C. The legend of the fall of Troy is such a memory, although the Greeks thought of it as a myth.

Where true and remembered historical events were concerned, these might be masked, so that the struggle between the Greeks and the barbarian Persians might parade as a battle of gods and giants — the primeval forces of nature — or of Greeks and Amazons. Greek art of the Golden Age comes no closer than this to reality. There is one great exception to the rule: a "frieze" runs along the top of the outer wall of the Parthenon behind the columned porch. On it is depicted the Panathenaic procession. This was a ceremony in which the citizens of Athens mounted the Acropolis to present a robe, specially woven by the young women of the city, to the ancient olive-wood figure of Athena in her temple. And here we see the people of Athens themselves, forming up for their march, driving sacred cattle, and bearing offerings. But again unreality steps in. The people of Athens are all youths and maidens of perfect beauty (Plate 7), and in the panels on the front of the temple they meet with the gods themselves, comfortably seated and awaiting their arrival. This is not, then, a true depiction of a historical event, and in a way the Panathenaic procession was not a historical event at all, but a religious one.

The ideal figures of Greece's Golden Age show no emotion. Like the portrait bust of Pericles, they regard the world with total, ideal serenity. Do they capture the true spirit of historic Greece? Not at all. Beneath this mask of serenity seethed a frightening reality. Athens had turned the Delian League into an Athenian Empire and her allies resented it bitterly. They united behind Sparta in rebellion, and Greece was plunged into a war that devoured almost seventy of what might have been the brightest years of her history. As the very temples of the Acropolis were being built, the country around Athens was ravaged yearly. The Athenian public was

7. *Procession of Maidens:* from frieze of the Parthenon, Athens, 447–432 B.C. *Paris, Louvre.*

fickle and unjust, constantly sending its leaders into exile and electing others. Phidias himself was accused of embezzlement and impiety by political enemies of his friend Pericles, and died in prison the very year, 432 B.C., his Parthenon sculptures were completed. Athens was eventually crippled, as was her victorious enemy Sparta, and the Golden Age came to a shameful end. But perhaps the eternal figures of Athenian art tell us more of the Athenians' true character than could a thousand turbulent scenes of battle; they tell us of the Greeks' all too human, striving for perfection, which is also peace.

8. Praxiteles. *Hermes with the Infant Dionysus*, about 350 B.C.
Olympia, Greece, Museum.

This *idealism* did not outlast the end of the fifth century and the days of
Athen's supremacy. After the Athenians lost political power, important
art was to be found elsewhere in Greece and not in Athens alone. And this
art of the fourth century was more natural. Likenesses of old age and ex-
pressions of laughter and grief began to appear, even on the faces of
mythical beings. It was as if the Greeks had given up hope of perfection.
The figures of the gods still displayed great, although more natural,
beauty. The flesh of *Hermes* by Praxiteles (Plate 8), the foremost sculptor
of the century, is softer and more real than that of earlier figures. The

cloth draped over the stump that supports Hermes comes so close to the appearance of real cloth that when the sculpture was first discovered and photographed, scholars who saw the picture thought that the archaeologist's workmen had carelessly left a piece of real cloth behind. But somehow the figure has less strength than the great nudes of a hundred years before.

The city-states of Greece were broken by constant wars, and when peace finally came, toward the middle of the century, it came too late. The barbarous Macedonians to the north, ruled by their king Philip, had speedily adopted Greek civilization and soon seized Greece itself. And it was Alexander, the son of this extraordinary ruler, who carried Greek culture and Greek art to the borders of the known world. Alexander mounted a small but well-trained force, taking philosophers and artists with him, and set about destroying the Persian enemy once and for all. From 334 B.C. until his death in 323 B.C., at the age of thirty-three, he conquered province after province until, having taken Egypt and the entire Near East, he finally reached the Ganges. Alexander's generals divided up his empire, and Hellenistic art — as Greek art of the period of Alexander was called — was the art of their courts. Faces of the ideal Greek type were to be found under the stylized traditional headdresses of Egyptian mummies; muscular Greek forms are to be seen in ancient Afghan and Indian reliefs. This imprint remained long after the Greeks themselves had retreated.

Plate 9 shows us what is called the Alexander Mosaic from the House of the Faun in Pompeii. It is a Roman copy of a Greek painting of the late fourth century B.C., showing the Battle of Issus in 333 B.C. It was in this battle that Alexander first defeated the Persian King Darius and his large army by outmaneuvering them on rough ground. Here we see the heat of battle, with contorted figures in every agonized position, and the sky pierced by sharp lances. The Greeks knew the art of painting as well as of sculpture, even during the Golden Age, but almost none of their paintings has survived. Still we can see how well and freely they were able to portray the anatomy of men and horses, fully rounded in space and swiftly moving. In the center of this detail Darius stands, mounted in his war

9. Alexander Mosaic: from the House of the Faun, Pompeii, about 90 B.C. *Naples, Italy, Museo Nazionale.*

chariot. (He escaped the battle alive, but his family fell into the hands of Alexander.) This may be a fair portrait of the Persian king, and the painting also includes a portrait of Alexander himself.

With a new realism in art, portraits became popular. Alexander, in fact, took his favorite portraitist on campaigns with him, and the conqueror's lionlike head with curling locks was sculpted again and again. And so we see here the portraits of real men as they were at a historical moment in time. We shall see this often in the art of Rome.

While Alexander and his generals were spreading Greek culture throughout the East, an obscure tribe living on the Italian peninsula far to the west was growing in strength. These people, the Latins, who had established the city of Rome as their capital, were gradually extending their power throughout the whole of Italy and into Sicily. Here they came face to face with the Carthaginians, descendants of the ancient Phoenicians, whom they fought in several wars and finally defeated.

At the opening of the second century B.C., the Romans had a taste for foreign conquest and they turned their eyes to Greece, the center of civilization. By mid-century they had crushed the city-states' last struggle for freedom. But the invaders seemed more anxious to seize Greek culture than to seize Greek lands. Roman gods were promptly identified with Greek gods, and the myths and legends surrounding the latter were adopted. Roman governors and administrators were greedier for Greek works of art than for gold; every movable statue, vase, or artistic object of any sort was packed off to Rome, where it was copied again and again. Many works, like the *Doryphorus* and *Diadoumenos* of Polycleitos, are known only through such Roman copies.

Latin plays were produced on Greek subjects in the Greek style, and poetry was written in Greek meters adapted to the Latin tongue. Finally, Greek philosophers, artists, and physicians were brought to Rome, and every wealthy Roman had a Greek tutor for his children. The Roman equivalent of a college education was a trip to Greece. In the words of the Latin poet Horace, "Captive Greece took captive her rude conqueror."

The Romans were not, in fact, all that rude. Long before the conquest of Greece they had met with Greek culture when they overran the Greek colonies in southern Italy and Sicily. Moreover, the Romans had inherited much from the Etruscans, their mysterious neighbors to the north. These strange people were both superstitious and violent, with a love of gorgeous luxury and a constant sense of tragedy. It was said that they accompanied every act with the sound of music, and they were deeply convinced that their civilization was fated to last just one thousand years and then come to a dreadful end. In their art we can see the influence of Greece. This only adds to the mystery, because they were not a Greek or Greek-speaking people (their language has never been clearly understood). But they do not seem to have been native Italians either, and where they came from remains a mystery.

But what about the Romans themselves? What were they like, these world conquerors? Thanks to a most peculiar custom, which they probably inherited from the Etruscans, we have a very good idea.

The Romans practiced a strange form of ancestor worship. From earliest times they kept wax death masks of their ancestors in their homes, and on public occasions and at funerals they paraded, carrying and sometimes actually wearing these masks. This habit must go back to a very primitive time, long before the Romans became world conquerors, when they, too, believed in sympathetic magic. Thus the ancestor magically appeared in the procession, and the crowd was forcefully reminded of how distinguished the family really was. This worship of ancestors deeply colored the Roman character. A man was deemed worthy of holding office in accordance with how many of his ancestors had held office, and so Roman families developed into powerful clans like the Claudians and the Julians. Moreover, every Roman was expected to possess the ancestral virtues, inherited from the days when the Latins were simple farmers and life was harder: *gravitas*, or a sense of responsibility; *pietas*, or piety; and *frugalitas*, which means many things — discipline, energy, and good humor in the face of adversity. By the first century B.C., the more civilized Romans had replaced wax masks with portrait busts as realistic and telling as the masks had been; the Romans had perfected the art of portraiture as never before.

To be effective, these *imagines*, or portrait busts, had to be as realistic as possible. The Greek portraits of Alexander resembled Alexander, but any blemishes that he might have had did not appear. The Roman portraitists, however, were ruthlessly realistic. In Plate 10 we see a statue of a man wearing a toga, the carefully draped robe of the Romans, and carrying two busts of his ancestors. This is in fact three portraits rather than

10. Republican portrait: *Statue of a Man Carrying Busts of His Ancestors,*
early first century A.D. *Rome, Palazzo Barberini.*

one, and we feel, like the superstitious spectator at a funeral procession, that three men stand before us rather than a single mourner. All three have the lean, hard, tough faces of Republican Rome; they are men who left their farms to conquer their neighbors and then the world. We cannot doubt their *gravitas* or *pietas* or *frugalitas*.

Roman history is alive to us because we know the faces of the men who made it — the tough, bullnecked, and conservative Pompey (106 B.C.– 48 B.C.), the shifty and clever Caesar (100 B.C.–44 B.C.), and the manly and bluff Anthony (*c.* 83 B.C.–30 B.C.). Suddenly we come to Augustus (63 B.C.–A.D. 14), and we see a change. Augustus was a pimply boy with acne and a constant runny nose, who killed his own uncle, among others, and seized power when he was still in his teens. Having brought a final end to the Republic, he made himself emperor and ruled with surprising wisdom. He also decreed that statues of himself appear in every city of the Roman Empire. When we look at these, we can only suppose that the ugly boy grew into a fine and robust man (Plate 11). But as the years passed, this man grew no older. His features remained the same, with broad cheekbones and lean chin — no wrinkles appeared. In fact, Augustus had decreed himself a god, and as a god he felt he always had to be represented as perfect and without fault.

But the idealization we see in the portraits of Augustus did not last. The Romans were great gossips and they loved cozy reality. Later portraits, even of emperors, return to the former realism: we see the blunt, powerful features of the Emperor Vespasian (Plate 12), who was so resourceful he was called the Second Founder of the Empire, and the refined faces of Hadrian (Plate 13) and Marcus Aurelius (Plate 14), both poets and philosophers as well as rulers. And we are shocked to see the head of the late Emperor Trajan Decius (Plate 15) looking more like a Christian martyr than an emperor of Rome. It is as if, with a suffering expression, he were watching the fall of the empire.

As the Roman Empire grew, a class of wealthy individuals arose: businessmen, property owners, and officials who drew large sums from the provinces. Unlike the Greeks, these Romans built huge and sumptuous homes — town houses and country villas that were in fact private palaces.

11. Statue of Emperor Augustus: from the Villa of Livia, Prima Porta, about
A.D. 14. *Rome, Vatican Museum.*

12. Head of Vespasian, about A.D. 70. *London, British Museum.*

13. Head of Hadrian, early second century A.D. *Rome, Museo Nazionale Romano.*

14. Bust of Marcus Aurelius, about A.D. 175. *Rome, Museo Nazionale Romano.*

15. Head of Emperor Trajan Decius, about A.D. 250. *Rome, Capitoline Museum.*

16. *Perseus Freeing Andromeda:* from the House of Dioscurides, Pompeii. *Naples, Italy, Museo Nazionale.*

17. *The Landing of Odysseus:* from the Odyssey Landscape, first century B.C. *Rome, Vatican Library* (right).

Moreover, after the fall of the Republic, the palaces of the emperors were nothing less than small cities. The Golden House of Nero (A.D. 37–68) covered the entire area of one of the seven hills of Rome, with artificial-looking landscapes and lakes scattered among an endless succession of pavilions, and Hadrian's villa at Tivoli covered several square miles. These houses were crammed with sculpture and beautifully wrought objects of bronze and precious metals, and their walls were richly decorated with paintings. In Rome, art was created for private people to suit private tastes, not merely for the glorification of the state.

If we look at these paintings, we will see that the Romans always clung to the culture of Greece. They learned much of their exquisite technique from Greece, in addition to the several styles they developed on their own. Then, too, Greek mythology supplied the subject for scenes like that of Perseus, who had slain the Gorgon, freeing Andromeda (Plate 16), and for delicate and exquisite landscapes like the painting of *The Landing of Odysseus* (Plate 17). The Romans never really fully understood perspec-

tive, but they attempted it, and they were probably the first people in ancient times to depict fully open landscapes in which the eye can wander freely. The Romans were the first ancient people to express true love of nature, and the quiet landscapes of Italy appear again and again in their poetry.

But in Roman wall paintings we find other subjects as well — above all,

18. The Garden Room: from the Villa of Livia, Prima Porta, first century B.C./first century A.D. *Rome, Museo Nazionale Romano.*

the daily lives and surroundings of the Romans. Plate 18 shows us the Garden Room of the Villa of Livia at Prima Porta. Here the wall has seemingly been made to open out onto a delicious garden, full of birds, flowers, and fruit trees, and we almost feel we can smell the jasmine in the air. In another painting (Plate 19) we see a simple kitchen scene, with pewter vessels, a dish of eggs, and game hung to age — tiny thrushes to be cooked

19. *Still-life with Eggs and Game:* from the House of Julia Felix, Pompeii, first century B.C./first century A.D. *Naples, Italy, Museo Nazionale.*

20. Wall painting from Nero's Golden House, first century A.D. *Rome, Museo Nazionale Romano.*

as one of the highly seasoned dishes that the Romans were so fond of.

Plate 20 is a corner of Nero's Golden House itself, painted in another style favored by the Romans — a simple and delicate architectural decoration. We can only be appalled at the character of Nero, whose artistic taste was said to have been excellent, and yet who was quite capable of burning Christian martyrs alive or feeding them to wild beasts in the arenas. But this extraordinary combination of exquisite refinement and brutality in many ways sums up the Roman character.

Unlike the Greeks, the Romans were concerned with the here and now. Their public monuments were decorated with reliefs of historic events and even minor daily events of public interest, such as the *Ceremony of the Census* (Plate 21). This relief, dating from the days of the Republic, shows the Censor registering and inscribing the citizens of Rome, stiffly carved in deep relief with no great skill. But with the emergence of the empire, the decoration of public buildings began on a grand scale, and the Romans became masters of narrative relief, with one scene following another to recount to the public an entire event from beginning to end.

The masterpiece of Roman art was the *Ara Pacis*, the Altar of Peace, erected by Augustus and dedicated in 9 B.C. It was built to celebrate the pacification of Gaul and Spain. The Romans, who now ruled a vast em-

21. *Ceremony of the Census:* from the Altar of Domitius Ahenobarbus, late first century B.C. *Paris, Louvre.*

pire, hoped for eternal peace in a world ruled sensibly, they felt, by Rome. This was to be the *Pax Romana*, the Roman Peace.

On the two long sides of the square altar we see scenes of the procession of vestal virgins, senators, priests, and officials, including Augustus and his family, that took place on the day of consecration. On either side of the east and west doors are idealized scenes of figures representing peace and prosperity. Here is true Roman realism. The figures are beautifully modeled and superbly draped, and their anatomy, the grace with which they move, is perfect. Those in the background are in more shallow relief than those in the foreground, giving a sense of depth. These reliefs might remind us of the Panathenaic procession of the Parthenon, but one glance will tell us they are very different. Idealized Romans do not stand before us, like the idealized Greeks of the Parthenon. These are actual portraits of those Romans present, frozen in marble, exactly as they appeared on July 4, 13 B.C. In Plate 22, we see Augustus himself and his family, all easily recognized. A child, probably his grandson, Lucius Caesar, is bored with the procession and tugs at the emperor's toga, while the man behind him pats the child's head and tries to quiet him. Elsewhere we see a woman with her finger to her lips, quieting a couple who are chatting. Augustus is portrayed, not as a god, as he would appear later in his reign, but simply as one among many. All is quiet dignity, but it is the dignity of real people.

The Roman Peace was far from perfect. In Plate 23 we see the *Triumph of Titus* from the first century. It celebrates a bloody moment in history. Alone among the people of the empire, the Jews of Palestine could not bow down to an image of the emperor as god or accept the Roman law, which they felt was inferior to their own. When they rose up to cast the rulers of the world out of their small territory, the bulk of the Roman legions was called in to crush the rebellion. The siege of Jerusalem was one of the most hard-fought in history, and when in A.D. 70 the rebels were defeated, fighting to the last man, their temple was sacked and destroyed and its holy relics were carried in triumph through the streets of Rome. It is this procession we see here, the most brilliant statement of Roman might in stone. Never has a mass of people been portrayed better in relief. By the clever use of light and shadow the sculptor has given the scene a

22. Processional frieze: from *Ara Pacis*, the Altar of Peace, 13–9 B.C. *Rome.*

23. *Triumph of Titus:* from the Arch of Titus, about A.D. 80. *Rome.*

sense of great depth; relief has never come more close to painting in effect. One feels as if one were looking not at a flat and sculpted wall but into the open air.

The *Pax Romana* meant peace for all those within the empire who did not rebel, but by the second century A.D. the emperor was regularly chosen by the army from among its generals, and the commander-in-chief emperors continued to extend the empire by waging war against the barbarians at its borders. And so the Column of Trajan (Plate 24), dating from the early second century A.D., celebrates war, not peace. Spiraling around the column is a continuous relief showing in episode after episode, like one continuous roll of film, the glories of Trajan's campaigns against the Dacians in what is now Rumania. Twenty-five hundred figures are to be seen on this seemingly endless scroll, 800 feet long. On it we see Romans embarking on ships, building fortifications, fording rivers, marching, sacrificing, hearing the emperor and receiving envoys, fighting and taking prisoners — the entire work of war. The figures seem large in proportion to the ships and cities they encounter, but this is necessary to squeeze a long and complicated story into a fairly small space, and the story of conquest with dignity and justice is brilliantly told. It was under Trajan (*r.* A.D.98–117) that the Roman Empire reached its greatest limits, stretching from Britain to Egypt, from the Atlantic Ocean to the outskirts of Asia Minor.

The column of Marcus Aurelius, which depicts the *Massacre of the Barbarians* (Plate 25), was erected at the end of the second century, and now we see a distinct change. This column was also decorated with a running frieze, an account of the emperor's victories on the Danube. The figures seem pudgy here, less well-proportioned than those of *Trajan's Column*, and the drapery of their clothing is carelessly expressed in hard, incised lines rather than carefully sculpted in deep folds. But most important, the spirit of the work has changed. The scenes are confused and the true, ghastly brutality of war appears, without its glory. The barbarians are massacred, the ground is strewn with headless corpses, and faces are twisted in tormented agony. We can perhaps sense the impending disaster — the empire was under attack.

24. Column of Trajan (detail), early second century A.D. *Rome*.

In their narrative reliefs, we see the Romans' pride of empire, their sense of their mission to rule the world and bring Roman culture, Roman justice and peace to peoples united by their dominion. Their hopes were never entirely achieved, and by the third century their empire was breaking up. Rome could not afford the heavy machinery of government for so large an empire, and time and again the army mutinied while its leaders struggled for imperial power. The undefended borders were attacked as wave upon wave of barbarians from the north and east penetrated deep into the Rhineland, Gaul, Greece, and Asia Minor. Cities were destroyed, trade shriveled, and whole populations were swept away, killed by the invaders and the epidemics that came in their wake.

If we look at a relief, *Constantine Distributing Largess* (Plate 26), from the Arch of Constantine, dating from the fourth century, we will see a row of squat, seemingly stiff little figures in flat and wooden drapery, with nothing whatsoever of the human energy or engaging realism of the *Ara Pacis* or *Trajan's Column*. Constantine, seated above the crowd like a god, is distributing largess. But now, as we shall see, in place of the Roman imperial power to inspire art there is a totally new spirit — the Christian faith.

25. *Massacre of the Barbarians:* from the Column of Marcus Aurelius, about
A.D. 180. *Rome.*

26. *Constantine Distributing Largess:* from the Arch of Constantine, about
A.D. 313. *Rome.*

1. *The Breaking of Bread,* early third century A.D. *Rome, Priscilla Catacomb, Cappella Greca.*

II

The ART of
the MIDDLE AGES

For three hundred years, Christianity was a forbidden religion. The Christians formed a secret society with their own private symbols — the fish, for example, because the letters of the Greek word for fish, *ichthys*, represented the initials in Greek for the phrase "Jesus Christ, Son of God, Saviour"; the shepherd, representing Christ himself; and the peacock with its many-eyed tail, representing the all-seeing God. The only ceremonies of the early church were the Baptism, and the Breaking of Bread in memory of Christ's Last Supper; these were held in the deepest secrecy. The Christian dead were buried in a maze of fetid underground tunnels, or catacombs, and here the living met by the light of flickering lamps to perform their religious ceremonies.

It was under these circumstances, fraught with immediate danger, that the first Christian artists worked. They covered the damp walls of the catacombs with paintings they hoped would give some comfort to their suffering brothers. Occasionally these artists were professionals, but for the most part they were amateurs; what they wanted to achieve was not the beauty of decoration, but the pure spirit of their religion, which they hoped would inspire others in the face of terrifying persecution.

The Breaking of Bread (Plate 1) is such a painting, dating from the early third century A.D., when time and again Christians were given the choice of worshiping the emperor as God or suffering a horrible martyrdom. We can see that this work is in the style of many other Roman wall paintings, but it has something the others do not. There is a certain human feeling as the communicants regard each other with tenderness and affection; this is rare in the classical art of Greece and Rome. The artist seems to have caught with a gesture, a tilt of the head, something

2. *The Good Shepherd*, mid-third century A.D. *Rome, Lateran Museum.*

of Christian love. Were it not for this, the scene might be that of a Roman dinner party. The confusion is deliberate. Early Christian artists painted scenes that might be taken by the casual observer to be the usual Roman decoration; this artifice was necessary for secrecy. If the catacomb was discovered, only the initiated Christian could recognize the symbols of his faith.

The shepherd was another favorite Roman subject. The familiar figure carrying a sheep on his shoulders was common even in the earliest art of Greece. Only a Christian would know that the shepherd in Plate 2, seemingly a typical Roman boy, was in fact the Good Shepherd who laid down his life for his sheep. Statues of this kind are rare, however, because Christian artists usually avoided free-standing sculpture. To them, a free-standing statue was too much like the images of an emperor, to which they refused to bow down no matter what the torture.

All this secrecy came to an end when the Emperor Constantine recognized Christianity with the Edict of Toleration, also known as the Edict of Milan, in A.D. 313. Christians could now come together openly in meetinghouses or in churches that were often merely reconverted Roman basilicas. (Roman temples were unsuitable for the Christian faith; they were built so that ceremonies could be held on the steps before their portals, with the mass of the worshipers outside, not inside, the building.) Moreover, when Constantine was later converted to the Christian faith and in A.D. 330 moved his capital from Rome to the small Greek city of Byzantium, which he called Constantinople, he changed the entire course of Roman history. Because of the constant pressure of invading barbarians, the empire could no longer be ruled from one capital alone. The choice of Byzantium in the East was a brilliant one; the city was perfectly suited for defense and, standing between the Mediterranean and the Black seas, it was in an ideal position for trade. The Roman Empire, however, was now not only Christian, but was forever split into two rival sections.

For the moment, the Roman world was part pagan and part Christian, and the confusion is nowhere better seen than in art. A good example of this state of affairs is the tomb of Constantine's half sister Constantia, now the Church of Saint Constantia. In a mosiac on the ceiling (Plate 3), we

3. *Constantine and Wine Harvest*, mid-fourth century A.D. *Rome, Church of Saint Constantia.*

see a portrait of Constantine surrounded by cupids, cheerfully harvesting grapes from intertwined vines, piling the grapes in carts, and treading on them. This simple decoration has been a source of mystery for centuries. Is this a Roman scene of the grape harvest, or does it have deep Christian meaning? Christ said "I am the true vine, and my Father the husbandman. . . . I am the vine, ye are the branches." The vine had become an important symbol of Christianity. Constantia lived and died a pagan, however, and she was buried in a typically Roman tomb. It was not until almost a thousand years later that she became a saint, and her tomb a church.

Many Christian churchmen wanted to keep the classical spirit alive in Christian art, but its inspiration was gone and another had taken its place. The ideal beauty of Greek art was no longer necessary or even in keeping with the spirit of Christianity. The events of this world and the immediate

4. *Christ Surrounded by Saints*, about A.D. 530. *Rome, Church of Saint Cosmos and Saint Damian.*

realism of Rome were equally unnecessary and even contradictory to the needs of the Christian faith. Christians were to look to the hereafter, to the eternal teachings of Christ. They were to turn away from earthly beauty and wealth toward spiritual goodness. In the words of an early Christian author, "They spend their existence upon earth, but their citizenship is in heaven."

In the two hundred years between the mosaics of the tomb of Constantia and the mosaic of the domed apse of the church of Saint Cosmos and Saint Damian (Plate 4), we can see that a great change has taken place. The saints in the foreground appear dressed as Roman senators, but that is the only resemblance to Roman art. There is less grace and naturalism, but a great deal more spiritual power than in much of Roman art. For almost the first time, the figure of a bearded Christ appears exalted on high.

The figures are stiffly frontal. They meet the viewer face to face and there is no way to avoid a confrontation — "and the Lord spoke to Moses face to face, as a man is wont to speak to his friend." The very technique of the mosaic itself, and its brilliant color, are new and different. The powerful religious meaning of the scene, the importance of the teachings of Christ, toward whom the apostles gesture, cannot be doubted. Many of these artistic changes came from the East, from Constantinople.

We have already spoken of how the Roman Empire declined during the third century A.D. It eventually recovered, but the population of the cities, decimated by barbarian invasion and plague, was never replaced and the towns became ghosts of their former selves. Craftsmen did not pass on their skills and their arts were lost; among these craftsmen were the painters and sculptors of classical Rome. The great landowners retreated to their estates, where the fields were tilled by forced labor and where small-scale industries coped with the owners' needs. The Roman Empire was now ruled from two centers, neither of which exercised the great central power of the earlier Rome. Of the two, Constantinople was the more prosperous.

The Eastern emperor was rich from trade, even if he did not control a territory of vast size, but his government had become a rigid dictatorship, more like that of ancient Persia than of Republican Rome. There was still a council called the senate, but it was no more than a puppet of the emperor, who was all-powerful. Only a few high officials were allowed into his august presence, and they were obliged to prostrate themselves. The simple toga of the Roman emperors was exchanged for a robe stiff with woven gold, and the Eastern emperor, like the kings of Persia, wore a jeweled crown. The very pavements were dusted with gold.

The art of Byzantium, as Constantinople continued to be called, was like the state itself — rich and rigid, more Persian than Greek or Roman. Horace, the Roman poet, spoke of *Persicos apparatus*, meaning the elaborate, overdecorated dress of the Persians. In Byzantium, this love of gold, jewels, and rich detail completely replaced the clean lines of Greece and Rome.

When we think of Byzantium, we think of the art of the mosaic, which the Byzantines perfected as never before. In a way these mosaics are the symbol of their love of wealth and display. Mosaics were common in Greece and Rome, where bits of marble and pottery were embedded in cement. But such effects were not sufficiently showy or extravagant for Byzantine artists. To the usual array of many-colored stones and pottery they added pieces of brilliantly colored glass — set at an angle to catch the light and glitter all the more — along with bits of gold and silver (often in the form of foil set between layers of glass) and even precious stones. Now backgrounds of dull white were replaced with brilliant blue, green, purple, and even gold. The effect of the display was to leave the viewer thunderstruck.

A mosaic of the Emperor Justinian (A.D. 527–565) and the Empress Theodora is from the Church of San Vitale in Ravenna (Plate 5). Justinian and Theodora were as bizarre a pair as ever held a throne, and their reign left a deep imprint on the history of art. Justinian was a brilliant ruler who codified Roman law, drawing its many conflicting regulations into a neat compilation that remained the basis of European law for centuries, and in some countries to this day.

Justinian's wife, Theodora, the daughter of a bear-feeder in the circus, had been an actress, then considered a low profession. Justinian married her after repealing a law that senators could not marry women who followed the stage. The result was the rule of one of the most ruthless and fascinating women in history. Theodora instituted a moral reform of the city and at the same time championed the rights of unfaithful wives against outraged husbands, who often put them to death. She was famous for her wit, but she never felt safe; she was severe, she had many enemies, and the city was full of her spies. Yet she had boundless courage. In 532, the Nika riots, which started as a squabble between rival sporting colors at the great Hippodrome, or racetrack, of Constantinople, developed into a full-scale revolution. But when the rebels had seized power, Theodora refused to join her husband in flight. "The throne is a glorious sepulcher," she declared. Through her own machinations she put down the revolution, executing, it is said, no less than eighty thousand rebels in the Hippodrome, where they had gathered to celebrate their victory. It is this

5. *Theodora and Her Courtiers* (detail), mid-sixth century. *Ravenna, Italy, Church of San Vitale.*

woman — small, pale, and very beautiful, by all accounts — whom we see in the mosaic.

Strange as this portrait might appear to our eyes, it gives us some idea of Theodora's splendor. She wears a collar of huge pearls and gems and a diadem heavy with cascades of pearls to the breast. Theodora's chambers were decked with silver columns and silver tables encrusted with mother-of-pearl and ivory; curtains of purple (the dye was an imperial secret); and Chinese scent burners. Her throne was of solid gold; her coach, gold-plated; and in her garden, ibis, peacocks, and pheasants were guarded by bronze dragons. This love of the exquisite, the extraordinary, and above all the beautiful was completely Byzantine. In fact, it was another Byzantine empress, Theodosia, who originated the beauty contest, when to choose a wife for her son Leo, she invited to her palace the twelve most beautiful girls in the empire.

Much of Constantinople was burned during the Nika riots, and Justinian set about rebuilding the city according to his own staggering plans. Churches, hospitals, convents, palaces, baths, aqueducts — all were rebuilt on a stupendous scale. The dome was the chief feature of Byzantine architecture. It was a form imported from the East that was almost unknown to the Greeks of classical times, and used only sparingly by the Romans. Byzantine exteriors were severely simple, but the interiors, the dome itself, the walls, the floors — every inch of space — were encrusted with a blaze of Oriental color. There was a rich decoration of mosaic above, and below was a scheme of intricately contrasting slabs of colored marble — gray, green, and red cipolin; red porphyry; or dark green verde antique, among others.

It was typical of Justinian that when he constructed his great Church of the Holy Wisdom, Hagia Sophia, he wanted to build the largest dome ever constructed. Over a period of five years, ten thousand workmen carried out his wishes, and the final dome spanned an area 107 feet across, its interior plated with gold. It is said that at the church's consecration, Justinian made the boast of a Christian, not a Roman, emperor: "Oh, Solomon, I have outshone thee."

But why were the famous portraits of Justinian and Theodora to be

6. Mosaics in the Presbytery, mid-sixth century. *Ravenna, Italy, Church of San Vitale.*

found at Ravenna, in Italy, far from Constantinople? Ravenna had, in fact, become the capital of the Western Empire under the Emperor Honorius in A.D. 402. It was later occupied by the barbarian Ostrogoths and was finally seized by Justinian himself, who reconquered Italy and for a short period made the Roman Empire once again whole. He then undertook at Ravenna (Plate 6) a building program that might vie, on a smaller scale, with his colossal plans for Constantinople.

But if Byzantine power and Byzantine art spread as far to the west as Ravenna, it spread much farther to the east. By the sixth century, Greek was the language of the court at Constantinople, and the power of Byzantium and the Byzantine church spread throughout the Christian settlements of the Near East. As the barbarous nomads of the Russian steppes were converted to Christianity, they too fell under the power of the rulers of Byzantium, and the princes of Kiev conducted a small imitation of the court of Constantinople.

For almost a thousand years, Byzantium remained petrified, unchanged in any way, incapable of innovation, as a seemingly nameless succession of emperors, bearded and stiffly robed, succeeded each other amidst the usual squabbles, intrigues, and conflicts that were no doubt loud, but which have been hushed by history. There were no real changes. Byzantium's art, too, was petrified, ruled by inflexible law and custom. The Madonna in Plate 7 dates from twelfth-century Russia, but it might have been painted centuries before. The expert, of course, knows that it was not — painting was rare in earlier Byzantine art, and during the seventh and eighth centuries the human figure was hardly ever portrayed. But the spirit remains unchanged. The flat, motionless frontality of the figure, and the great, dark, brooding eyes, which to the Byzantine artist represented communion with God — these are the same. Moreover, we see this Madonna often, inclining her gentle head toward a Christ child formed like a small adult, his drapery falling into a pleasing pattern having nothing to do with the natural folds of cloth. This was a stock figure repeated again and again in the Byzantine East and especially in Russia. (Such religious portraits, painted for churches on wooden slabs, were called *icons*, or "likenesses.") So it was that, until the sacking of Constantinople by the Turks in 1453, the Roman Empire of the East remained as if frozen in place; and as generation upon generation of scholars copied texts to which they added little, the best of Roman and Greek literature remained frozen with it, awaiting the great thaw of the Renaissance.

Meanwhile, Western Europe was undergoing a tremendous and painful transformation. After A.D. 476, the Roman Empire in the West was no more. Invasions of the Germanic Sarmatians, Goths, Lombards, and many others spread into Italy, France, Spain, and England, pushing the native Celts ever westward into Brittany, Cornwall, Wales, and Ireland.

The invaders did not inhabit the cities they destroyed, and the world of the Roman Empire with its cities and towns disappeared once and for all. These primeval European peoples, the Celts and Germanic tribes alike, had their own art, an art which had existed before the coming of the

7. *Our Lady of Vladimir*, about 1125. *Moscow, Tretyakov Gallery.*

8. Gold buckle: from the Sutton Hoo Treasure, seventh century. *London, British Museum.*

9. Purse: from the Sutton Hoo Treasure, seventh century.
London, British Museum.

Romans and which continued to exist. Naturally, as they did not live in settled communities, these people had no use for large-scale painting and sculpture; their art had to be portable. And so they decorated small and valuable objects with great skill, lavishing their love of design on their jewelry, their weapons, and the trappings of their animals — symbols of wealth and power they could easily carry with them.

Every inch of space on the gold buckle in Plate 8 is covered with an intricate pattern of interlacing bands. Barbarian craftsmen loved to experiment with endless meandering lines, forming circles and triangles, scrolls and knots, like the intertwining of tendrils, leaves, and boughs in the thick forest that had been their home. And, as in a forest, their designs are sometimes populated with small human and animal figures. These figures are stylized to appear at one with the flat patterns of the decoration: the little animals and men on the purse in Plate 9 are a perfect example.

Often a figure of a man is framed by two lively animals in what later became a heraldic pattern; this theme must be very ancient. We can only admire the fineness of the gold and enamel work in these plaques and admit that the craftsmen who made them were serious artists in a society that must have put a high value on their work.

Both the buckle and the purse are from the Sutton Hoo treasure found in the remains of a ship in which an Anglo-Saxon chieftain was buried, not at sea, but on a cliff overlooking a river in East Anglia. This warrior was laid to rest, along with all the possessions apparently most dear to him, in the seventh century. So little is known of this period that it is called the Dark Ages, but we can assume that the barbaric tribesmen were slowly settling on the land and adopting Christianity. They were not all learned. But small groups of churchmen were setting out, mostly from the East — brave and determined little knots of men from Syria and Egypt — establishing monasteries in Italy, on the coast of France, and in faraway Ireland. They brought with them books and the learning of the Church and the art of Rome and Constantinople.

Much of Europe was covered by forests, where wolves and wild boars ran free. Men lived in wattle hovels within the wooden stockades of local chieftains, where all alike sat and slept on straw. A wooden chair, a coffer, these were scarce and precious objects; and a single suit of clothing might last a lifetime. Fields were plowed, cloth spun and woven; everything was done by hand. Above all, the church had a tremendous task to perform. The Gospels had to be taught and taught well to a people who were almost totally illiterate.

In the sixth century, Pope Gregory saw that there was only one way in which this could be done: "Painting could do for the illiterate what writing can do for those who can read." Art, then, was to be the language in which the stories of the scriptures were to be taught to millions of the faithful — people to whom religion was to be the deepest inspiration, and the will of God their entire reason for existence. To the churchmen of the Eastern empire, the use of works of art for religious purposes always smacked of the idol worship of pre-Christian Rome. This is why, like the earliest Christians, the artists of Byzantium created no sculpture. But to the church of the West, art was all-important in every form — wall frescoes, statues, heavily decorated objects of every kind, and illustrated manuscripts. When few, even among the clergy, could read, books consisting of the written page alone were not enough. The texts had to be heavily and lavishly illuminated, literally "lit up" with illustrations, the meaning of which was beyond doubt.

There is something touching about the tale of such clergymen as the Abbot Benedict Biscop in seventh-century England, who traveled back and forth to Rome — a trip by tiny boat across the English channel and then a journey of many months through savage or hostile territories — to bring a few precious manuscripts all the way to Britain. There, as elsewhere in Europe, these invaluable holy books would be painstakingly copied by generations of monks. And if the words were copied, letter by letter, so were the illustrations, sometimes line for line. Originality was not important for the nameless medieval artist. What was important was that every story be readily understood. If a certain apostle appeared dressed in a certain way, then he must always appear in that way, so that he could be recognized immediately by any viewer. In fact, pattern books existed so that any illuminator could discover immediately how any subject was to be interpreted; these pattern books were handed down from generation to generation.

Let us look at two pages from such early manuscripts — pages from the time we call the Dark Ages. Plate 10 is taken from the *Codex Amiatinus*, an early eighth-century copy of a text dating from late Roman times. Here we see the figure of the Prophet Ezra, seated at his bookcase and busily writing. The anatomy of the figure seems natural and the whole scene is shown with some knowledge of depth and perspective; in fact, all the techniques of the Roman wall painters of classical or early Christian times are repeated under the influence of the rich, flat patterns of Byzantium.

Now let us look at a page from the *Lindisfarne Gospels* (Plate 11), painted shortly afterward. We have stepped into the Dark Ages. In painting Saint Matthew, the artist has not tried to be original. Clearly he is copying the same pattern for a seated, writing figure as the artist who painted the Prophet Ezra. But here there is no anatomy, no depth. The entire picture forms a flat pattern. The drapery falls in folds that are more decorative than natural and the figure seems stiff, unable to move. But this does not mean that the picture is any less dramatic in meaning. Far from it. In a way, Saint Matthew reduced to a scheme of flat colors seems all the more vivid to us, and this may be because we sense something of the deep faith of the artist himself.

10. *The Prophet Ezra:* from *Codex Amiatinus*, about 700.
Florence, Biblioteca Laurenciana.

And so we have the art of Rome, crudely remembered and stiffly reinterpreted by the Byzantine East, combined with the barbarian love of interlacing design we see everywhere in the picture — on the bench, in Saint Matthew's robes, and in the four corners of the composition — to produce richly decorated books with much painstaking labor. These pictures are not memories of the past; they are memories of memories. And yet they were given a new life and vitality and were clung to as if all civilization depended on them, as it very nearly did. In the words of

11. *Saint Matthew:* from the *Lindisfarne Gospels,* early eighth century. *London, British Museum.*

Zoë Oldenbourg in her book *The Crusades:* "The average [medieval] man was able to tell his direction by the stars and the movement of the sun, had a sure hand and eye, was wise in the lore of plants, and carried in his head an accurate calendar. . . . For theoretical knowledge he relied on old men, travelers' tales, professional story tellers, and the sermons of the parish priest. . . . " In such a world these precious manuscripts carried the weight of the whole Christian religion and encompassed all history and philosophy — the sum of human knowledge, such as it then was.

Gradually, throughout Europe, the feudal system was taking root. Peasants became increasingly tied to the land as they exchanged their freedom and much of their harvest for the protection of some local warlord or chieftain. Protection was needed in a world where marauding hordes and greedy neighbors made a habit of seizing whatever land was not well protected and life was an endless struggle for which the faithful were rewarded only after death. Clearly a leader was needed; that leader appeared in A.D. 768 when Charlemagne, Charles the Great, became King of the Franks, the most powerful barbarian people on the European continent.

A seven-foot giant with a fierce temper, who wore homespun on principle and fathered fourteen children, Charlemagne succeeded in conquering much of Europe in a series of bloody campaigns. But this barbarian was above all an idealist. His was to be the new Roman Empire, built along Christian lines, a Holy Roman Empire with all the peoples of Europe united under him and God, in a lasting peace. At Aachen near the Rhine, between present-day France and Germany, Charlemagne tried to build a court that befitted the splendor of his notions. He constructed a large palace and chapel (Plate 12) built in the Byzantine style of stone, used for the first time in northern Europe since Roman days.

12. Palace chapel, about 800.
Aachen, Germany.

Charlemagne's plans were endless; he was a man many centuries ahead of his time. Although it is possible that he himself was illiterate, he saw to it that his daughters as well as his sons were taught to read, and he wanted to establish universal education throughout his empire. Of course he attracted the finest artists to his court, the most skilled craftsmen, and the most brilliant intellectuals. Antique art was collected and "scriptoria" were established — writing rooms in which manuscripts were copied on a large scale and script itself was revised and simplified.

Travelers and merchants and ambassadors brought to Charlemagne's new capital a constant flow of rich and beautiful objects from every corner of Europe and the Near East. Much of the treasure of Byzantium literally fell into Charlemagne's lap. When he crushed the Avars, a tribe from the Russian steppes, who had served the emperor of Byzantium as mercenaries, he seized a vast hoard of Byzantine silks, ivories, and works of silver and gold. Moreover, the Iconoclasts, the "image smashers," a religious sect that abhorred the creation of human likenesses, came to power in Byzantium, and the artists of Constantinople fled to Western Europe, bringing their techniques with them. Riches from farther east, too, poured into the capital at Aachen when the Caliph of Baghdad arrived, accompanied by caravans loaded with damasks, jewels, spices, and perfumes, along with a water clock and an elephant. Everything that could be studied and copied was copied, and the eyes of Europe were opened.

If we look at the work of the artists of Charlemagne's court school, we can see how close the grizzled old warrior actually came to re-creating a Roman Empire. Compare, for example, the Saint Matthew in Plate 13 with the seated figures in the earlier manuscripts we have seen. Here is a true return to the painting of ancient Rome. The depth, the careful shading, the knowledge of anatomy, the full sweep of naturalism, all are here. In the workmanship of the ivory cover of the *Lorsch Gospels* (Plate 14), we see figures cloaked in delicate and swirling drapery, and it is as if the long-forgotten art of Christian Rome had literally sprung back to life, united with the very best the Byzantine artists had to offer.

After the death of Charlemagne his empire was split among warring

13. *St. Matthew:* from the *Coronation Gospels,* early ninth century. *Vienna, Schatzkammer.*

14. Ivory cover of the *Lorsch Gospels*, early ninth century.
   London, Victoria and Albert Museum.

factions and an era as dark as what had gone before settled back on Europe; it was darker, in fact. Works of art in the flat stylization of the years before Charlemagne reflected the universal gloom. Earlier Christian art had avoided scenes of pain and suffering, but now the agonies of Christ were depicted in moving detail (Plate 15).

Meanwhile, beneath the surface, an organized society was taking shape. Feudalism hardened and the difference between peasant and nobleman became more defined in law and even in dress. Peasants were now obliged

15. *The Crucifixion:* from the *Otto II Gospels*, about 980.
Aachen, Germany, Cathedral Treasury.

to wear simple garments of drab color and uniform size so that they could immediately be distinguished from the brightly dressed nobility at a glance. Larger and larger areas were ruled by a single power, and powerful local rulers united to form kingdoms of some size. This was the world of the myths that later came to be called fairy tales, where rulers might lose their power in an instant, where pagan spirits were still believed by the common man to roam the earth, and where so little was known of the world at large that a young man setting out to "seek his fortune" was likely to encounter strange and unimaginable adventures.

But where there was more organization there was greater prosperity. There was now more trade than ever before and there were more specialized craftsmen: carpenters, weavers, goldsmiths, silversmiths, and the like. And where there was a demand for trade and the work of craftsmen the tiny, sheltered communities of peasants who worked the fields became towns.

After the year 1000 a new energy seemed to infuse the people of Europe. The Church was all-powerful and the deeply religious population now had the wealth to express its fervid faith by building larger and more beautiful houses of worship; huge cathedrals of stone took the place of small wooden churches. Towns vied with one another to produce the most magnificent of these cathedrals and the local nobility discovered the advantages of building stone castles and fortifications for their protection. And so, during the eleventh and twelfth centuries, in one great wave of activity, Europe was turned from a world of wood to a world of stone.

The new churches and cathedrals were planned on a scale larger than anything attempted since Roman times. Now they needed to accommodate not only growing communities but also hordes of pilgrims — groups of the faithful who traveled throughout Europe and beyond to visit sacred places — such as the site of a miracle or the burial place of a saint. The world was in many ways a more open place than it had been for centuries. It was now, too, that the churches of Europe finally took the traditional cruciform, or cross, shape, with a central nave, and transepts that crossed the main section at right angles. Behind the altar the area called apse was extended to make room for several altars and the relics of saints. Most important, the architects were anxious to roof their splendid buildings with durable stone rather than timber, which easily caught fire, and so they experimented with the problem of the vault, a ceiling or roof supported by intersecting arches.

Today the style of this era is called Romanesque. On these Romanesque churches the people of Europe lavished whatever skill, craft, wealth, and faith they had. In them, colorful rows of columns supporting circular arches are embellished with every imaginable design. Flowers, vines, human figures, and animals, real and imaginary, peep from every corner

16. Romanesque pulpit, second half
of twelfth century. *Palermo, Sicily,
Cappella Palatina.*

17. *The Commission to the Apostles,*
tympanum, about 1130. *Vézelay,
France, Church of La Madeleine.*

(Plate 16). All of them tell a story. In fact, Romanesque churches have been called "storybooks in stone." The story that they tell is, of course, the story of Christ, and with the Romanesque church the art of sculpture was reborn in Europe.

In Plate 17 we see a page from a medieval manuscript translated into stone — *The Commission to the Apostles,* which appears over the portal of the Church of La Madeleine at Vézelay, France. Christ is clothed in the weightless, swirling drapery we have seen in the illuminated manuscripts, and he floats above the apostles whom he is sending forth to preach throughout the world. Round about are scenes representing the nations that were to receive the Gospel, including the pygmies of Africa and the cynocephali of India, dog-headed people of medieval fancy. Above all, we sense a deep expression of emotion. Christ blesses with hands outstretched; and these hands, one of which is missing, are the most important feature of the composition. They are deliberately exaggerated, far larger in proportion than they should be. The expression on Christ's face is one of exalted holiness and spirituality. We see that same expression on the face of the crucifix in Plate 18.

18. Romanesque crucifix (detail), about 1070. *Essen-Werden, Germany, Abbey Church.*

19. *Storm on the Sea of Galilee:* from *Hitda Gospels*, early eleventh century. *Darmstadt, Germany, Landesbibliothek.*

It is in Romanesque art that the deepest and most passionate sentiments are felt. Everywhere emotion is let loose; even the sail of the ship in the *Storm on the Sea of Galilee* (Plate 19), an illustration from the *Hitda Gospels*, shows the flaming emotions of a divine force as the ship itself seems to prance through the waves.

The walls of the Romanesque churches were covered with paintings, and again the church was a storybook. Often *Christ in Majesty* (Plate 20) was portrayed in the apse, facing the Last Judgment at the other end, so that the worshiper felt a clear choice between salvation and damnation. Scenes from the Old and the New Testaments ranged along the sides and vaults of the church. In these we see the same flat pattern of decoration, the same swirling free lines, and the same imagination we have seen in the illuminated manuscripts. In Plate 21 — a wall painting of the *Annunciation to the Shepherds* — animals, both real and imaginary, prance at every angle around a landscape of branching trees. There is no realism, but there can be no doubt of the meaning of these pictures. In the painting of *Adam and Eve Working* (Plate 22), the figures are seen against an imaginary pattern of soil and vegetation. Medieval man saw the first man as living a life not unlike his own. Adam and Eve are dressed in furs, but Adam breaks earth with a hoe and Eve spins thread with a spindle of the sort that must have been a common sight in the twelfth century.

Medieval man loved symbolism of every kind. Animals, plants, the figures in certain stories, all symbolized something of deeper importance, and colors themselves held symbolic meaning. Red represented both love and hate, and brown was the color of poverty, decay, and the renunciation of the world. Black, of course, was the color of evil, death, and the Devil, and blue represented heaven, heavenly love, and truth. Blue was also the color of the Madonna. These colors were everywhere in the Romanesque church; even the sculptured relief was painted. Such ·color was particularly important in a world where dyes for clothing and paint for furniture were far beyond the reach of the common man. During the long, cold winter, the Church provided most of the people of Europe with the only color they saw, and this must have added much to the shock and excitement of their religious experience.

20. *Christic in Majesty:* from the Church of Saint Clement, Tahull, 1123. *Barcelona, Spain, Museum of Catalan Art.*

21. *Annunciation to the Shepherds* (detail), about 1150. *León, Spain, Saint Isidora, Panteón de los Reyes.*

22. *Adam and Eve Working:* from Sigena Monastery, twelfth century. *Barcelona, Spain, Museum of Catalan Art.*

Slowly, slowly, medieval man was beginning to focus not only on the hereafter and on the many spiritual personalities of the scriptures, but on himself. Here and there among the many sculpted figures that thronged the Romanesque churches the common man in his drab dress was to be found, often busy at the "Labors of the Months," the typical work of each season, such as plowing, sowing, and shearing. And, in fact, the common man had become the artist. Now sculptors, mural painters, and even the illuminators of books were often professionals rather than merely members of a local monastic order. These professional artists traveled from town to town, spreading their styles and tastes.

But in the eleventh and twelfth centuries, despite the growth of towns and the building of churches and cathedrals, men's minds were still in darkness, their world a frightening place where death was ever-present and eternal punishment was at hand at every moment. Again and again, artists repeated scenes of the suffering of Christ, and devils and demons lurked and hissed from every corner of the village church or town cathedral. Not until men's minds were finally truly opened by the great adventure of the Crusades and other historical developments did fear gradually lose its grip.

From 1096 until 1291, Christian armies repeatedly attacked the East. Their object was to drive the Mohammedans form the Holy Land and to put the holy places at last in the hands of the Christian church. This seems a strange course for a poor, backward, and illiterate society with its eyes turned always to heaven, but there were many reasons for it. For one thing, the Arab world had threatened Europe with invasion for centuries. Mohammedan powers had seized Spain and Sicily as well as taking lands from the weakened Byzantine Empire. When the Seljuk Turks captured Jerusalem from the more peaceful Arabs of Egypt and virtually cut off European pilgrims from the holy places, Western Christian armies lost their patience. Moreover, Europe was not so poor or so backward that Europeans did not feel the need for a more direct means of trade with the East and they went in search of it. But most important, the Church had struggled for centuries to curb the warlike spirit of the barbaric noblemen by forming councils to keep God's peace. Now the love of battle could be turned to Christian purpose. Pilgrimages were a form of penance, and the barbarian warrior, heavy with sins, could find salvation by performing a sacred pilgrimage under arms and by taking up his sword to fight universal evil rather than his neighbor.

In practical terms the Crusades meant that vast armies of men in full European armor shambled over huge distances to suffer famines and plagues before they even met their "Saracen" enemies, as they were called. And still there was no lack of recruits. Who were these men? They were warlords in search of new territories, younger sons who would inherit no title or property, traders, criminals, bankruptees, adventurers of every kind, and men yearning to burst the restricted confines of medieval Europe, to start a new life, to see the wealth of the East about which they had heard in their chilly and uncomfortable homes. They left their wives and families for years and even decades, the majority never to return. They were no different in many ways from the men who later explored the New World or tried their luck in the gold fields of California. So vast was the movement that the Crusaders were not content to set up camps, but constructed European castles in the crackling heat of the desert and built whole cities along their routes.

What success the Crusaders met with was short-lived, but the effect of the Crusades on Europe was enormous. As men were killed abroad, properties changed hands at home, and feudalism was shaken at its foundations. European rulers established trading colonies in the East, and along the routes cities developed to handle the ever-growing trade; among these cities were Venice, Genoa, and Bruges. But most important, the Crusaders who set out with their eyes on the other world returned with their eyes open to a new world on earth. From the East they brought back new plants and fruits such as lemons, melons, and sugar; new cloths such as cotton, damask, and muslin; new fashions and refinements such as powder and glass mirrors. They brought back, too, a new interest in history, a new knowledge of mathematics, and a realization of the poetry of their struggle. New myths and legends were created. Above all, the Crusaders became aware of the existence of a world outside Europe. Asia was opened up and Europeans, like the Polos of Venice, went as far as Cathay. Meanwhile, there was such a flock of tourists to the Holy Land that guidebooks were written and package tours were made available.

The artists' eyes were opened, too. In Plate 23 we see, not some mythical monster from the medieval imagination, but a real elephant, carefully observed and drawn. The artist was Matthew Paris; we have his name and know something about him. He was a monk at Saint Albans Abbey near London, and he had not, in fact, traveled in the East, but had observed an elephant that arrived in London as a present from Saint Louis (Louis IX), King of France, to Henry III. As Matthew Paris explained, "From the size of the man drawn here one can get an idea of the size of the beast."

Now, in the thirteenth and fourteenth centuries, art was created for

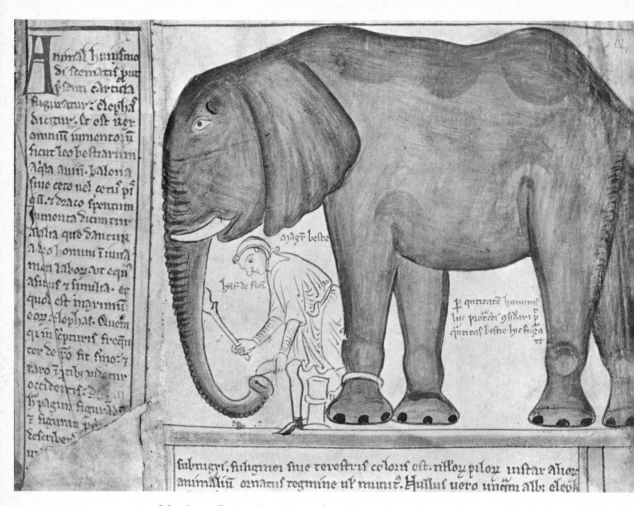

23. Matthew Paris. Drawing of an elephant: from *Chronica Majora*, 1255. Cambridge, England, Corpus Christi College Library.

a wealthier, more worldly society than had existed since ancient times, and a new style, called Gothic, developed. The word "Gothic," like the word "Romanesque," has changed its meaning many times, but in art today it refers to a style that first developed in France in the middle of the twelfth century and dominated the next two centuries throughout most of Europe, although Romanesque styles were still in use.

It is thought by some that Gothic art began with the ideas of a single man, the Abbé Suger (*c.*1081–1151), abbot of Saint-Denis, just outside Paris. The abbot was a worldly man and a lover of beauty in all its forms.

He wrote, "It is only through symbols of beauty that our poor spirits can raise themselves from things temporal to things eternal." In other words, look hard at the beauty of this world; it is the only way you will be able to grasp the beauty and eternal truth of God — a far cry from the other-worldly faith of the early Christians, whose "citizenship" was "in heaven."

But what is most important is exactly what Suger did to create visual beauty when he set about the reconstruction of the burial place of the kings of France — the abbey Church of Saint-Denis, the patron saint of France. Here Suger and his architects put three new elements of design to use: the pointed arch, the ribbed vault, and the flying buttress. All had been used somewhere in Europe before, but to combine them was a stroke of genius. The pointed arch could span a far greater width and achieve a greater height than the earlier round arch. Moreover, the ribbed vault, with its solid ribs reinforcing the arch, could carry an even higher ceiling, bearing stresses that were supported not by thick walls, but by flying buttresses outside the structure — props of arched stone that carried the weight of the high vaults to solid outside pillars of stone.

High above the heads of the faithful a heavy stone ceiling could now be supported, held by tall, narrow pillars, and the wall space between could be replaced by brilliantly colored windows. The churches and cathedrals built in this Gothic style after Saint-Denis strove, each one, to be higher, lighter, and more ethereal than those that had gone before, so that the soul of the worshiper was literally wafted aloft in an ecstasy of pure beauty that reached ever heavenward (Plate 24).

Such changes in taste, the new search for beauty, would not have been possible if the society of Europe, too, had not changed. Wealth and the ability to buy physical comfort and objects of beauty changed the very way men were able to think. The attractions of this world were now not only apparent, but within the grasp of a good many people. As trade developed, a whole class of citizens in the towns, the merchants (the *bourgeoisie*, as they were called in France), were able to earn money and to spend it. More and more people learned to read and write and there were opportunities that had never existed before outside the Church — opportunities for craftsmen and men of learning.

24. Cathedral nave, first half of thirteenth century. *Amiens, France.*

Life was far more comfortable than it had been previously. The nobility in their castles and the townsmen in their well-built homes enjoyed the luxuries of windows, carpets for the chilly floors, and tapestries against the drafty walls. They slept on comfortable beds with mattresses, sheets, and blankets. Life was softer, and a new humanity, a love of elegance, flavored everything, and most especially art.

As ever, the local cathedral was the pride of the community. Because the cathedral made the town a commercial as well as a religious center, the merchants — along with the local nobility, the church, and every able-bodied man — contributed what they could to its construction. And as ever, the churches were richly decorated with sculpture so that their walls, their portals, and their interiors appeared like a lacework, originally a highly painted lacework, of sculptured detail (Plate 25).

25. North transept portals and porches, twelfth century. *Chartres, France, Notre Dame Cathedral.*

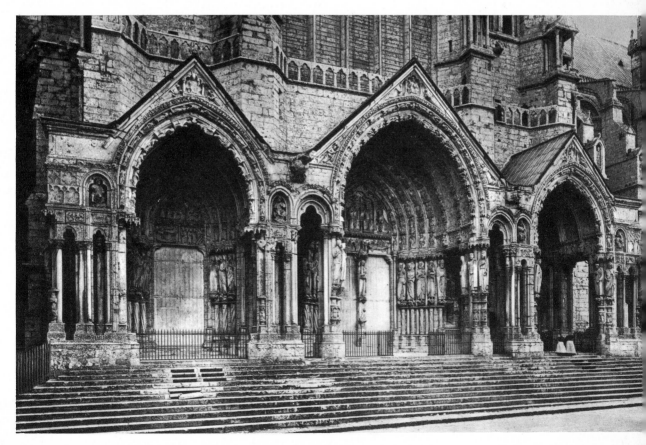

If we look at *The King and Queen of Judah* (Plate 26) from the west façade of the Cathedral of Chartres, we see at once that, even though the figures are elongated to complement the columns of which they are a part and even though their drapery falls in flat, contrived folds, they are still more natural than anything we have seen in the art of the Middle Ages. Their anatomy appears rounded and human beneath their garments, and the face of the queen has a vivid everyday realism. In the Cathedral of Rheims we see figures, their proportions close to reality and their drapery falling more naturally, that stand almost free of the wall (Plate 27). These changes are most striking in the little ivory group depicting *The Descent from the Cross* in Plate 28. Here, without looking like the classical models, the anatomy of the delicate figures has been captured perfectly by the sculptor. The drapery seems composed of some cloth that is at once both soft and stiff; it is still the decoratively draped cloth of medieval art. But most important, the deep drama of the scene, the broken body of Christ borne from the cross, is all the more touching because the figures are natural.

This naturalism led to the creation of portraits; often rulers and those who contributed to the construction of cathedrals and churches could be gratified by the sight of their own faces on the figures at the portals. The head of a youth in Plate 29, for example — from Henry III's palace at Clarendon, England — could not be anything but a portrait of a beetle-browed individual. And there is an almost scientific naturalism in the fruits and flowers that decorated the columns of church interiors (Plate 30). But all this love of visual realism did not detract from the thirst for beauty, and often the figure of the Virgin (Plate 31) now appears more like a pretty, painted doll than the mother of Christ.

Because much of the wall space in Gothic cathedrals was taken up by huge windows, wall painting was complemented by windows formed of brilliantly hued glass. The art of stained glass was a technique that had been known in Byzantium, but now it was carried to new heights. Leaded into grids of geometric form, the windows now told long tales with hundreds and even thousands of figures, their details painted right onto the tiny fragments of glass. The effect was of a ravishing mosaic of jewels

26. *The King and Queen of Judah:* column
    figures from the west façade,
    twelfth century. *Chartres, France,
    Notre Dame Cathedral.*

27. Figures of saints and prophets: from the west façade,
    about 1240. *Rheims, France, Cathedral.*

28. *The Descent from the Cross,* second half of
    thirteenth century. *Paris, Louvre.*

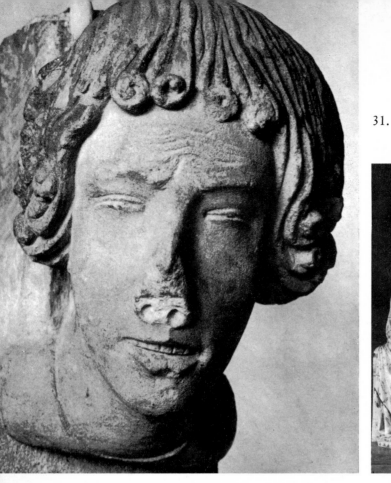

31. *Coronation of the Virgin,*
about 1260. *Paris, Louvre.*

29. Head of a Youth: from Henry III's Palace, Clarendon, Wiltshire, about
1240. *Salisbury, England, South Wiltshire and Blackmore Museum.*

30. Capital from passage leading to the
Chapter House, late thirteenth century. *Southwell, England, Minster.*

that filled the interior of the cathedral with brilliantly colored light
(Plate 32).

But wall painting was not dead as an art. The walls of the private palaces of local rulers were often covered with biblical scenes of rousing
warfare. The painted wood panel of the Westminster Retable (a ledge

behind an altar) gives us some ideas of what these wall paintings must have been like (Plate 33). Here Saint Peter's drapery is light and rippling, and yet the figure is molded with knowing shadow. Above all, it is painted with a delicacy and refinement, an *elegance*, that are altogether new. It is this love of elegance that is the key to Gothic art and to something new in the Gothic mind.

32. *Good Samaritan Window* (detail), early thirteenth century. *Chartres, France, Notre Dame Cathedral.*

33. Saint Peter: detail from the Westminster Retable, 1260–1270. *London, Westminster Abbey*.

The fact is that the minds of men in the thirteenth and fourteenth centuries were no longer taken up with religion. Just as a love of hunting had begun to replace the traditional love of warfare among the nobility, so the Code of Chivalry and the Code of Courtly Love had stepped in to distract the imagination of medieval men. The Code of Chivalry was the result partly of the necessary comradeship of the Crusades and partly of the structure of the thirteenth-century world. To retain a position of nobility, to win or hold possessions, a young man of noble birth was required to have a certain training. It was necessary for him to become a knight. In order to do this, he would be sent by his family to the court of his father's liege lord, the most powerful prince or nobleman of the district, to serve for several years as page and to learn the arts of fencing, archery, and hunting. His mind was trained, too, and he learned to write poetry. Above all, he was imbued with a sense of honor. He was trained to defend his lord, the cause to which he was sworn, and all innocent members of the female sex no matter what the risk. After four years of such training he might be promoted to the position of squire, and as such might follow his master into battle as a servant. Then, if all went well, at the age of twenty-one he would be admitted to knighthood.

During all this period he might admire the ladies of the court, but only from afar. Even when he was a grown man, his marriage would be arranged on a basis of property, and if he were without funds he would be obliged to win possessions with his sword before he could hope to finance a noble wife. Under such conditions it is not surprising that love from afar, love quite outside the bonds of matrimony, should have become the custom. This custom was celebrated by the troubadours who traveled from court to court reciting the poetic "romances," often heroic tales taken from the mythology of the Crusades. According to the Code of Love, "love never lives in a house of avarice," and "the true lover is always shy," but also "marriage is not a legitimate bar against love," and "there is nothing to prevent a woman being loved by two men, or a man being loved by two women." The young knight who rode into the tourney with the colors of his love on his sleeve did not have his mind set on the spiritual teachings of the Church.

Of course, chivalry and courtly love crept into art. In a way, the lovely doll-like Madonnas of the age were in fact the ideal woman, the true object of courtly love. But art was no longer confined to religious works. Now that more members of the nobility and the wealthy bourgeoisie could read, there was a great demand for illuminated books, not all of which were devotional. The romances and the historic lays were illustrated as the scriptures had been, and were eagerly read. In Plate 34 we see *The Capture of the Cross by Saladin*, a tale of the crusades from the *Chronica Majora*, a history of England by the same Matthew Paris who painted the historic elephant of Henry III. And in Plate 35 we see Tristram and Yseult, courtly lovers in the truest tradition: King Mark of Cornwall welcomes his nephew Tristram as his guest and heir, but after drinking a potion, Tristram falls in love with Yseult, King Mark's betrothed and later his wife, Tristram and Yseult are fated never to be joined and die in each other's arms.

Such tales were avidly read by women as well as men. It was an extraordinary age in that, while women generally held a low legal status, they were venerated by the Code of Love, and were often educated. During the Crusades, with their men away, women of the nobility were obliged to defend their property on their own initiative. Some of them were among the toughest generals of their age. There were women poets, weavers, merchants, and doctors, and women directed great trade enterprises; in Paris alone there were women practicing more than a hundred professions.

Apart from romances, another favorite form of illuminated manuscript was a kind of calendar in which the work of the various seasons of the year was carefully depicted. Perhaps the most famous of these to survive is the book called the *Très Riches Heures* of the Duc de Berri. The duke, an extraordinary lover of the arts, collected a vast treasure of jewels, objects of art, and manuscripts in his palaces. On each exquisite page of the *Très Riches Heures du Duc de Berri*, life in Gothic France and the pastimes of noblemen and peasants alike are depicted in the most exquisite detail. In the portrayal of April (Plate 36), courtiers are entertaining themselves in the country, and we see that the artist is now observing everything closely.

34. Matthew Paris. *The Capture of the Cross by Saladin:* from *Chronica Majora*, about 1250. *Cambridge, England, Corpus Christi College Library.*

35. *Tristram and Yseult on a Bench;* and *Tristram and Yseult in the Love Grotto:* from *Roman de la Poire,* about 1260. *Paris, Bibliothèque Nationale.*

These are no longer flat figures on a flat background. The artist knows nothing of the laws of perspective, but he has observed how all things — grass, leaves, the fading blue of the sky — look at a distance, and there is a remarkable sense of depth. The castle in the background is no doubt genuine. Many of the scenes and locations painted in the *Très Riches Heures* have been identified. The artist has observed, too, the rich texture of the courtiers' robes. The world the Limbourg brothers have painted for us in this book is very different from the crude, brutish life of the earlier Middle Ages. The slender, elegant figures with their voguishly high waists are in the height of fashion.

But this picture could be a fashion plate. In fact, the age was fascinated by luxury and fashion. Women might be covered with jewels from head to toe and they used a variety of techniques to improve their beauty. To remain fashionably slim, they devised a kind of Turkish bath; they whitened their skin with leeches and colored their hair with henna, saffron, or calf's kidney. The days of the simple, rough wool tunic were long gone. If a fashion for a new cut of sleeve, a new kind of headdress (a vast variety of hats were worn) was started in Paris, within a few years it might reach as far as the Norse colonies in Greenland, where the settlers, literally dying from starvation, would copy it in detail. At one period the pointed motif of Gothic architecture was adapted in clothing, and men and women alike wore pointed shoes, pointed sleeves, and pointed hats in such exaggerated form that laws to limit them were passed. A nobleman could wear shoes with points only two feet in length; for the wealthy bourgeoisie, one foot was allowed; and for commoners, a half foot.

Such laws against extravagance are called sumptuary laws, and they became common. The Pope forbade long trains, pearls, and gold and silver braid, and the King of France, Philippe le Bel (Philip IV), limited the size of a noblewoman's wardrobe to four dresses, while bourgeois wives were to wear no ermine, squirrel, gold, or precious stones at all. Trains were so long that one bishop harangued, "If women had needed tails, God would have provided them." All this said a great deal for what trade and the textile industry had done in bringing comfort and luxury to Europe. It also said a good deal for what had become of the power of Christian teachings and the Age of Faith.

36. Pol, Hennequin, and Herman de Limbourg. *April:* from the *Très Riches Heures du Duc de Berri*, begun 1415. *Chantilly, France, Musée Condé.*

In this last stage, the Gothic style in art is called International Gothic, and it was in fact international. Although France assumed the lead, the examples we have seen were taken from far afield. The Christian Church was still all-powerful and it still united Europe. Latin was still the language of the Church, and the international language; art and architecture in the Gothic style, with strong local variations, were to be found from Germany to Spain and from Italy to England. But this unity was the unity of the Church, and the Church was losing its grip on the minds of men. New forces were afoot, and already in Italy changes were taking place. There would not be another international style for five centuries.

III

The RENAISSANCE

AT THIS VERY MOMENT, while the artists of the Gothic north were refining their exquisite technique in a limbo between worldliness and saintliness, the ancient civilization of Rome was reborn, and with it what we call modern civilization was born, in Italy.

Why did this Renaissance or rebirth take place in Italy? Italy had lagged behind and the great strides in learning had been made in the north. Gothic art had never really taken root in most of Italy, where artists clung to the old Romanesque or Byzantine styles. Italy, moreover, was in permanent political chaos. The south, the Kingdom of Naples, was ruled by a foreign monarch who was also the Holy Roman Emperor. The emperor battled endlessly with the Pope at Rome for control of Italy, and life was one continual war. The cities in the north were controlled by no one at all and fought ceaselessly with the emperor, with the Pope, and with each other.

The entire peninsula was divided into two rival factions: the Guelfs, who supposedly sided with the Pope, and the Ghibellines, who were thought to side with the emperor. The Guelfs and the Ghibellines walked differently, greeted one another differently, dressed differently, and even cut their bread differently, but there is little evidence that they actually thought differently, even on political matters. They simply fought. In a local dispute over the possession of an olive tree, one family would claim to be a Guelf, its opponents would take the side of the Ghibellines, and they would fight. Hélène Nolthenius in her book *In That Dawn* describes the state of affairs in Italy: "In the northern cities men went to war because they liked to: there was always the hope of having a good time." This hardly seems the atmosphere in which great new ideas are formed, and yet it was.

Why? There are several good reasons. During the thirteenth century the feudal nobility in Italy had become so weak that the peasants, tortured by marauding bands of robbers, fled in vast numbers to the cities. The great cities of northern Italy, Florence, Pisa, Pistoia, Arezzo, Milan, Cremona, Parma, and Bologna, grew as no cities had grown since the days of ancient Rome. From the mid-eleventh to the mid-thirteenth century the population of Florence grew from six thousand to seventy-four thousand. Milan and Venice were one hundred thousand strong. Moreover, these cities were free and democratic; no local feudal lord in his rural castle could hope to control such a population. The children of the bourgeoisie were educated as were few princelings in the north, and the guilds, the organizations of every profession from judge and banker to slaughterer, were powerful. Every man who owned property had a hand in the government. And the towns, although they fought one another, would always unite to defend their freedom against any potentate, be he emperor or pope. In 1287 the city of Milan had no less than 3,000 mills, 1,345 churches, 1,000 taverns, and 150 hospitals. In such a setting it is not surprising that new ideas should take root.

Moreover, Italy, at the great crossroads of trade between East and West, North and South, was influenced from many directions. In the south, the Kingdom of Naples was settled by Arabs, Jews, black Africans, Greeks, Normans, Germans, and Spaniards. As late as 1270, decrees were published in Latin, Greek, Hebrew, and Arabic (Italian was not yet recognized as a language). In the north, Venice, the greatest trading city of Europe, had defeated Byzantium and actually ruled large areas of Asia Minor. The sumptuous buildings and churches of Venice were neither Romanesque nor Gothic; they were a fantasy of Byzantine domes and mosaics.

One influence, the most important, lay buried in the soil of Italy itself. Medieval Rome was a shambles. One traveler, Huillard-Breholles, recorded that "The heat is unbearable, the water is foul, the food is disgustingly bad. You can cut the air with a knife, for the whole place swarms with gnats and scorpions. The people are dirty and disagreeable, spiteful and unfriendly. The whole city in fact is undermined with the catacombs, which are full of snakes and all the time emit poisonous fumes." The great families, the Frangipani, the Pierleoni, the Orsini, and the Colonna, feuded with one another and with the Pope, who was time and again driven out and then invited back. Meanwhile, the huge Baths of Caracalla sat in the middle of a swamp, vegetable gardens were cultivated around the Pantheon, and in what remained of the Roman Forum, cattle stood munching their cud. The princes of Rome used these ruins to quarry blocks of marble for their palaces, but otherwise the ruins of ancient Rome stood unnoticed. It was the same throughout Italy.

Perhaps the first true Renaissance man was Frederick II (1194–1250), the Norman King of Sicily. He was also the Holy Roman Emperor, and so his possessions surrounded and engulfed Italy, and his rivalry with the Pope was keen. It was all the keener because Frederick, born and brought up in Sicily, was influenced by Hebrew and Arabic writings and questioned the teachings of the Church.

It sometimes happens that we come upon a completely modern mind entrapped in another age, and that was Frederick. He was interested in mathematics, natural history, architecture, and medicine. And above all, he questioned everything, possessing what we call a scientific mind. He bathed daily, and this alone was enough to establish his reputation for ungodliness, as frequent bathing was considered an unchristian indulgence of the body. He was fascinated by animals and their habits and always traveled with a complete menagerie of camels, leopards, exotic birds, bears, lions, and a giraffe. Falcons were his passion, and specimens were sought for him as far afield as Germany and Persia. He once gave a condemned man an opportunity to save his own life by scaling a dangerous cliff to capture a rare white falcon. An athlete — a famous diver — was sent to plunge into the whirlpool of Charybdis to find out what was at the bottom. Frederick's reply to the question "Did God give birds of prey their beaks and claws to harm other creatures?" was an answer worthy of Darwin. "No," he said, "but because they need them."

A questioning man like Frederick could not look at the remains of Imperial Rome and Greece strewn about his lands and simply forget them. He collected as many works of classical antiquity as fell into his hands. It is not surprising, then, that Nicola Pisano, whom many consider the first artist of the Renaissance, is thought to have come from Frederick's territories in southern Italy and to have visited his court.

With Nicola Pisano (*c.* 1220–*c.* 1278), we see the art of ancient Rome reborn with one stroke. In *The Nativity* (Plate 1), the composition seems confused and crowded. There is no sense of perspective. In good medieval fashion, the figures are large or small according to their importance, and several scenes take place at once. But let us look at the figures themselves. These are not the stiff, slender, fragile figures of medieval art. They are bulky forms of flesh and blood. And they are draped in thick cloth that does not flutter with a spiritual life, but falls heavily in natural folds according to the laws of gravity. These might be the powerful, muscular figures of ancient Rome, with their straight noses and severely even, classical features.

Nicola's son, Giovanni Pisano (*c.* 1245–*c.* 1320), with whom he later worked, seems to have been influenced by the sculptors of Gothic France. In *The Annunciation and Nativity* (Plate 2), we see scenes similar to Nicola's but much more crowded together. In the upper left the angel Gabriel tells the Virgin Mary that she will give birth to Christ; in the upper right the mother and child in the manger are adored by angels; in the foreground Joseph watches the child being washed. But the whole

1. Nicola Pisano. *The Nativity:* from the pulpit, 1260. *Pisa, Italy, Baptistery.*

composition is lighter and airier than those of Nicola, and more in the style of Gothic art.

At work with Giovanni Pisano in the Arena Chapel was the man who is called the father of Renaissance painting, Giotto di Bondone (*c.* 1266– *c.* 1337). Giotto was probably born in Florence and there is a story that the master painter Cimabue discovered him as a shepherd boy, drawing a sheep in the earth with a stick. In any case, Giotto was Cimabue's pupil, and Cimabue, like the other painters of his time, was conservative. His *Virgin and Child, Enthroned with Angels and Prophets* (Plate 3) is a flat Byzantine composition. It is not so very different from the Byzantine Madonna painted in Russia almost two centuries before (see Plate 7, Chapter II), although Cimabue's Madonna and alert Christ Child seem more human and individual.

If we compare this Madonna with Giotto's fresco *The Death of Saint Francis* (Plate 4), we can see what a huge step forward the younger artist has taken. (A fresco is painted on the wet, or fresh, plaster of a wall, so that the colors become part of the wall itself.) In *The Death of Saint*

2. Giovanni Pisano. *The Annunciation and Nativity* (detail): from the pulpit, 1297–1301. *Pistoia, Italy, Church of Saint Andrew.*

3. Cimabue. *The Virgin and Child, Enthroned with Angels and
Prophets*, about 1285. *Florence, Uffizi Gallery.*

4. Giotto. *The Death of Saint Francis* (detail): from the Bardi Chapel, about 1325. *Florence, Church of Santa Croce.*

Francis the figures are bulky and deeply modeled in shadow, and they move freely in space. They are not ideally handsome; they might have been men whom Giotto knew. Moreover, we sense the drama of the moment immediately; it is written on the faces of the mourners. One monk, his cheeks red with tears, kisses the saint's hand. Another is so horrified he throws up his arms in grief, while still another watches acutely for a sign of life.

Giotto is said to have been the first painter since antiquity to work from a living model rather than merely copying long-standing and accepted versions of a subject. Moreover, the scene must have been especially real to Giotto because Saint Francis, the beloved "Clown of God," had died not so many years before this fresco was painted. A wealthy young man who gave away all his possessions and preached poverty and joy in God's creation, Saint Francis had attracted thousands of followers throughout Italy during the thirteenth century, and his order remained an important counterbalance to the growing greed for material wealth.

In Giotto's *The Annunciation of Saint Anne* (Plate 5) we can again sense the drama of the scene as an angel flies through the window to tell Saint Anne of the coming birth of Christ. Again the figures are solid, naturally posed, and modeled in shadow. These figures are not the weightless, rippling forms of medieval art; they are planted firmly on the ground. In a way, Giotto was the first artist to bring his figures down to earth and into the realm of visual reality as men knew it. Giotto even noticed the little articles of everyday life in Saint Anne's house. The architectural setting is particularly interesting. Scale did not disturb artists of the early Renaissance any more than it disturbed medieval artists. Often a whole town appears in miniature so that the viewer may know that a town was there. In this case, Saint Anne's house is just large enough to contain the action of the scene, and Giotto has tried to paint it with a studied perspective. But let us look at the style of architecture itself. The roof is crowned with something that looks very like the triangular pediment of a Roman or Greek building, and below it runs something like a classical frieze. The whole miniature structure has the clean, foursquare proportions of a classical building. Clearly the remains of ancient Rome were

5. Giotto. *The Annunciation of Saint Anne,* about 1305. *Padua, Italy, Arena Chapel.*

being discussed and examined at the time, and Giotto appreciated them.

Giotto enjoyed great success. He was invited to work in cities from Naples to Venice to Milan, and he may even have gone as far as Avignon, in southern France. The Pisanos and Giotto's master Cimabue had also been famous; Dante wrote in his *Il Purgatorio:*

> Credette Cimabue nella pittura
> tener lo campo, ed ora ha Giotto il grido
> si che la fama di colui oscura.

> Cimabue thought he held the field in painting,
> but now all the talk is of Giotto,
> and the other's fame is obscure.

The sculptors and painters of medieval Europe were largely unknown, and even if their names were inscribed on their work, little was known of their lives. But now, the artist began to be appreciated as an individual, cities competed for his attention, and poets praised him. All this was part of the general interest and appreciation of man as an individual that was part of the change of outlook we call the Renaissance.

In fact, during the Middle Ages the arts themselves were not distinguished one from the other. Poetry was written to be sung, and was often accompanied by dance or mime. Painting and sculpture were not works of art on their own, but were part of an overall architectural design for a church or palace. But with the Renaissance each art form gained its own, individual importance. However, the artist was expected to be an expert in many fields. Giotto himself had a hand in designing the bell tower for the cathedral in Florence. As we shall see, it was many centuries before an artist could comfortably claim to be merely a painter or a sculptor.

During the Middle Ages the facts of nature were scarcely known and never questioned. There was one general answer to inquiry: "It is the will of God." If a scholar wanted to know something specific about animals, the weather, the sun, moon, and stars, there were always the authors of antiquity — Aristotle in particular — to supply the answers. But at the court of Frederick II, questions were bandied about: What causes fire to come out of volcanoes? Was Aristotle correct in maintaining that the earth is round? Why is some water sweet and some water salty? Why does an object half submerged in water appear bent? To answer such questions, Frederick had assembled at his court the best thinkers of his day: One of his scholars, Leonardo da Pisa, introduced Arabic numbers to the West.

The questions may not have been answered immediately, but they were asked, and many answers would be found during the next three centuries as scholarship and learning outside the Church blossomed and grew. Universities consisting of nonclerical students studying nonreligious subjects had existed as early as the ninth century in Italy and only slightly later in northern Europe. Now many such universities sprang up, especially in the towns of northern Italy. These were not universities in the modern sense. Often they consisted of nothing more than a famous teacher, or a few such, who had attracted a group of students. But to have a learned establishment was considered a matter of great pride to a town, and the competing cities of northern Italy offered a teacher and his students every comfort in an effort to attract them. The best food and lodgings were provided at low cost. Unfortunately, the students often repaid such hospitality by behaving so badly that the town eventually threw them out. But it was easy enough to find a hearty reception elsewhere, and by the late thirteenth century some cities were actually famous for the excellence of their universities in certain fields. The University of Salerno in Sicily was known for its medical teachings — learned from the Greeks, Arabs, and Jews, since care of the body was not a part of Christian concern. Students went to Bologna to study law, and to Paris for the study of theology. Students could go anywhere on the European continent since all subjects were taught in Latin.

Surprisingly, it was during this very period that the vernacular, the spoken languages, of Europe became written languages. Three of the greatest writers in all of Italian literature lived during the fourteenth century: Dante wrote his *Divine Comedy*, the great poetic account of heaven and hell; Petrarch wrote his sonnets, which were to be a model for all time; and Boccaccio wrote his *Decameron*, witty and biting tales of the life of his age. All three turned the jargon and street language of their day into language worthy of literature.

And yet, although they wrote in Italian and not Latin, these men were among the first and greatest of the humanists, scholars and writers who turned away from the Christian studies of medieval Europe to the pagan writings of ancient Greece and Rome. They called themselves humanists because their interest "was not in God, but in man," and these were the studies that Cicero, the Roman orator, had described as "human." Dante pictures himself being led through Hell not by another Christian, but by another poet, the Roman Virgil; and the personages from history he meets on his great journey through Purgatory to Paradise are not all Christian. Romans and Greeks are there among them; their stories are taken from classical mythology, then little known in Europe, but fascinating to the humanists. Petrarch imitated the forms of Latin poetry and wrote treatises on antiquarian subjects, and Boccaccio was famous for his Latin mythology, biography, and geography.

The works of Latin and Greek literature had always been known by scholars, but now reading and studying them became an obsession. Long-lost manuscripts were searched out from every corner of Europe and were avidly copied by armies of scribes. The dusty libraries of abbeys and monasteries from Germany to Spain were ransacked for lost works of Cicero, Lucretius, Statius, Plautus, and many others. Wealthy collectors paid fortunes for these manuscripts, more fortunes to have them copied, and still more to have Greek works translated into Latin, which all those who read could understand. The great Federigo da Montefeltro collected ancient books as a boy, and as Duke of Urbino amassed one of the largest libraries of his time. Moreover, popes were as interested in classical literature as were princes. Pope Nicholas V impoverished himself as a monk by buying manuscripts, and as Pope he collected nine thousand volumes, the basis of the Vatican library. When he moved his court to Fabriano because of the plague, he made certain to bring his scribes with him "to protect them from death."

Now the ruins of Rome attracted as much interest as Roman literature. Little by little, excavations were undertaken. The Roman art of wall painting was discovered, and works of sculpture were unearthed. As is usual in such circumstances, there was a fever for collecting. When asked why he traveled throughout the Mediterranean collecting inscriptions and sketches of ruins, Cyriacus of Ancona replied, "To wake the dead." Cardinals as well as noblemen filled their palaces with fragments of ancient statuary and claimed descent from noble Roman families. Pope Pius II, his gouty foot propped up, cheerfully had himself carried in a litter along the ancient roads to the ruins outside Rome. In his war against Naples he granted amnesty to the men of Arpinum because it was the home of Cicero. To the Italians of the fourteenth and fifteenth centuries, the long-forgotten glory of Rome became their most cherished heritage. It was this "rebirth" that gave the Renaissance its name.

But the men of the Renaissance did not take the writers of ancient Greece and Rome as unquestioned authorities in the way that the men of the Middle Ages had accepted Christian teachings without question. Renaissance men were interested in Latin literature because they wanted to know more about men and nature, and their interest did not stop with the words of ancient authors. They questioned these as they questioned everything. They pursued their investigations further.

The Italians of the Renaissance were great travelers, and in these centuries a traveler outside the bounds of Europe was necessarily an explorer. Even before Marco Polo accompanied his uncle to China and met the Emperor Kublai Khan, the Pope had sent Brother John of Plano Carpini on a similar expedition. Brother John got as far into Tartary as Karakorum. Like the Polos, he described strange and fabulous things, that were often, according to modern research, quite true, although he was scarcely believed in his time. And it was a Genoese who found the Canary Islands in the thirteenth century.

Except for astronomy, the natural sciences were not taught at the universities, but the atmosphere of the times was friendly to scientific inquiry, even if the Church was not. Botanical gardens were cultivated and every nobleman wanted to have specimens of every variety of plant in his gardens. Animals were collected, too. Horses were bred with great care, and the wealthy and powerful kept large menageries containing every known beast. Cardinal Ippolito de Medici even went so far as to keep a human menagerie, with peoples from Africa and Asia speaking no less than twenty different languages: Tartar bowmen, Indian divers, and whirling dervishes. Although the great scientific discoveries of Vesalius (1514–1564) in anatomy and of Galileo (1564–1642) in physics and astronomy did not come until the sixteenth and early seventeenth centuries, the groundwork had been laid by thousands of anxious and inquiring minds.

A questing scientific approach to reality and an admiration for Rome and what was known of Greece — these attitudes formed what we call the Renaissance. Both interests had a great effect on art. Of course, the expression of deep sentiment and inner truth had always been of great importance; the art historian Bernard Berenson has written in *The Italian Painters of the Renaissance:* "... As there were no professions scientific in the stricter sense of the word, and as art of some form was the pursuit of a considerable proportion of the male inhabitants ... it happened inevitably that many a lad with the natural capacities of Galileo was in early boyhood apprenticed as an artist. And ... [he] was obliged his life long to make of his art both the subject of his strong instinctive interest in science, and the vehicle of conveying his knowledge to others." And it was in Florence that a group of energetic young men began to study the art of antiquity and to discover how to translate the visual world onto canvas and into stone with the utmost scientific precision.

At the beginning of the fifteenth century, two young men set out for Rome together. One, Filippo Brunelleschi (*c.* 1377–1446), had just lost a competition for the commission to sculpt bronze reliefs for the doors of the Cathedral Baptistery in Florence. The winner had been another young man, Lorenzo Ghiberti (1378–1455), who collected Roman sculpture and regarded himself as an artist in the classical style, although his reliefs (Plate 6) still showed the depthless composition and weightless grace of Gothic sculpture. Perhaps it is just as well that Brunelleschi lost the competition; Ghiberti spent the rest of his life creating the doors for the Baptistery.

Brunelleschi's companion on the journey to Rome was the young sculptor Donatello (*c.* 1386–1466), hardly more than a boy. As soon as the two young men arrived, they set about examining every relic of an-

6. Lorenzo Ghiberti. *The Annunciation:* from the North Doors, 1403–1424. *Florence, Baptistery.*

7. Filippo Brunelleschi. The Pazzi Chapel, about 1429–1443. *Florence, Church of Santa Croce.*

cient architecture and statuary in the city. Brunelleschi had by now given up his work in sculpture to concentrate on architecture. Intent on imitating the builders of antiquity, he measured every ruin he could find, "to restore to light the good manner of architecture." What he achieved when he eventually returned to Florence can be seen in his façade for the Chapel of the Pazzi family (Plate 7) in the Church of Santa Croce. Here six Corinthian columns support an architrave in the classical style; pilasters (flattened columns) decorate the wall behind; and the front door is surmounted by a triangular pediment. But this is not a slavish imitation of Roman architecture. The columns are more slender and lighter than Roman columns; and the façade is built around an arched entrance. The total effect is something entirely new and completely Florentine. What often started in a spirit of imitation now became complete innovation. This then, was the *rebirth*.

Brunelleschi made another great contribution to art. He devised and set down the laws of linear perspective. How do objects appear at a distance in space? When drawing a box, the parallel lines appear to meet, but at what angle? The painters of ancient Rome grappled with the problem but never really solved it, and the artists of the Middle Ages did not even try. Giotto had approached the matter simply by observing objects carefully as they receded in space, but he arrived at no scientific law. Brunelleschi did. It was he who discovered that parallel lines as they recede in space meet at a common vanishing point.

Donatello examined the antique statuary of Rome with a passion: the sculptures' strength, their solidity and vigor, and the Romans' superb understanding of every muscle of anatomy. He digested all this and returned to Florence, although he came back to Rome many times to continue his

8. Donatello. *Saint George Killing the Dragon*, about 1417.
   Florence, Orsanmichele.

studies. He had already been a student of Ghiberti, but upon his return to Florence, he established a career of his own and very soon surpassed his master.

Donatello's innovations were many. As we can see in his *Saint George Killing the Dragon* (Plate 8), he adapted Brunelleschi's principles of perspective to relief sculpture; and on the right we see a colonnade that disappears into the distance, opening up the background of the scene in great depth.

Donatello's splendid figure of the great *condottiere* Erasmo da Narni, called *Il Gattamelata* (Plate 9), is the first equestrian statue (figure of a man seated on a horse) cast in bronze since ancient times. Donatello must have seen the equestrian statue of the Emperor Marcus Aurelius that now stands in the middle of Rome's Campidoglio. He had studied the painfully realistic Roman portrait sculpture, too, and on the *condottiere*'s noble and melancholy figure we see a head that is not beautiful, not ideal, but which has all the noble ugliness of a Roman senator. This form of sculpture became a favorite during the Renaissance, especially for portraits of the *condottieri*, mercenary leaders who fought for one prince and then another, often carving out empires of their own.

We can see in all these works that Donatello understood anatomy, but most revolutionary, most shocking of all, was his statue of David (Plate 10). Here finally is Donatello's tribute to the statuary of Rome and Greece. The biblical hero is shown as a slightly built youth, totally nude and leaning on one leg in the relaxed *chiasma* position of a Greek god. Christianity and pagan art had finally met.

9. Donatello. *Il Gattamelata*, 1443–1447. *Padua, Italy*.

10. Donatello. *David*, about 1435.
Florence, Museo Nazionale del Bargello.

11. Masaccio. *The Tribute Money:* from the Brancacci Chapel, about 1427.
Florence, Church of Santa Maria del Carmine.

The genius of the young Masaccio (1401–*c.* 1428) burst upon the world of painting as Donatello's did upon the world of sculpture. Masaccio (the name, derived from his first name Tommaso, means "hulking Tom") must have been something of a boy wonder, as he was a member of the guild of doctors and apothecaries, to which artists belonged, at the age of twenty-one. Brunelleschi's theories of perspective are more suitable to the art of painting than to relief sculpture, and it was Masaccio who brought the full depth of scientific perspective to his work. But he did much more than that. He filled his deep perspectives with atmosphere, with an interplay of light and shadow. And he used this light and shadow to model his figures deeply. If we look at his fresco *The Tribute Money* (Plate 11) we can see why Vasari, when he recorded Masaccio's life a century and a half later, said that "he rendered relief that was characteristic and natural, and that no painter had ever before attempted." Moreover, his figures have the sculptural solidity and anatomy of the statues of Donatello as they stand naturally posed and bathed in shadow. The drama of the scene is apparent immediately. With outstretched hand the toll collector demands to be paid. Christ sends Peter to take a coin from the mouth of a fish (left), with which the debt is paid (right). Christ is in all ways the focus of attention, and the human grandeur of the figures in their heavily falling drapery sets the standard for paintings of high seriousness for all time.

Masaccio died tragically at the age of twenty-seven, probably of the plague, although there is a legend that he was murdered. Some feel that had he lived he might have become the greatest painter of the Renaissance. But he achieved what he did when he was quite young; this is true of many artists of the time. The painters of Florence were a group of young men, many of them still boys. They knew each other; they befriended and hated each other; and they competed with each other, every one fired by the desire to find a way to re-create reality that was truer and better than any other. The artists of the next generations looked to Donatello and Masaccio for inspiration.

Some, like the Dominican friar Fra Angelico (*c.* 1387–*c.* 1455) were not really members of the group. It is said that Angelico was an artist

12. Fra Angelico. *The Annunciation*, 1440–1447. *Florence, Convent of San Marco.*

who happened to be a saint; certainly the good brother lived a quiet and modest life in his monastery, and his piety and devotion were above question. He was more conservative than Masaccio and the figures in his paintings seem to have the sweet and weightless spirituality of Gothic art. Fra Angelico was particularly known for his brilliant color — he actually mixed his paints with crushed jewels. It was said that he never painted a crucifix without tears streaming from his eyes. And yet Angelico's saintly figures are set against backgrounds of classical perspectives (Plate 12). He was among the first painters to discover that many different vanishing points could be used.

For Paolo Uccello (1397–1475) the study of perspective was a passion. His name means "little bird," and in fact he was so poor that he had to satisfy himself with paintings of the little birds he could never afford to keep as pets. But he studied perspective to the point of madness. Vasari, the sixteenth-century author of *The Lives of the Painters*, said that "he would have been the cleverest and most original genius since the time of Giotto if he had studied figures and animals as much as he studied and wasted his time over perspective." In fact, he studied nature so little that he produced a monument to the English *condottiere* Sir John Hawkwood showing the captain seated on a horse that moved both legs on one side. He was likely to paint horses green or pink quite deliberately.

Uccello's *Saint George and the Dragon* (Plate 13) is a strange, unreal decoration. The doll-like figures do not appear to be made of flesh and blood; they seem rather to be assemblages of geometric forms. Even the dragon's wings are an exercise in perspective, and the setting is made up of a series of perspective lines. Yet the entire scene has great charm — the charm of a fairy tale, but not that of a religious event.

Domenico Veneziano (*c.* 1400–*c.* 1462) was a very different kind of painter. His *The Madonna Enthroned* (Plate 14) is certainly made of flesh and blood, as is her baby; the figures could not fail to have a deeply religious appeal. Veneziano, too, employed perspective settings, and he too was an innovator. He brought daylight into these settings and studied atmospheric effects so accurately that the viewer is able to identify the hour represented.

13. Paolo Uccello. *Saint George and the Dragon*, about 1460. *London, National Gallery.*

The perspective of Uccello, the soft daylight of Veneziano, the solid anatomy of Donatello — all were combined in the paintings of Piero della Francesca (*c.* 1410/20–1492). His *The Baptism of Christ* (Plate 15) shows the dignity and monumental quiet that fill all his work with a deeply religious calm. And yet even Piero was preoccupied with perspective and wrote a treatise on the subject that shows close mechanical observation: "I say that a point is the smallest thing that an eye can recognize. And I

14. Domenico Veneziano. *The Madonna Enthroned*, about 1444. *Florence, Uffizi Gallery*.

15. Piero della Francesca. *The Baptism of Christ*, 1445–1450. *London,
National Gallery.*

will call a line the extension of one point to another, and whose width is of the same size as is a point."

The Pollaiuolo brothers, Antonio (*c.* 1432–1498), who was the greater artist, and Piero (*c.* 1443–1496), and Luca Signorelli (*c.* 1441/50–1523) applied themselves to the study of anatomy with almost as much passion as Uccello had to the science of perspective. They wanted, above all, to give to their figures the explosive energy that they must have felt around them. They made endless sketches of the nude human body in an effort to portray every possible contortion and movement, hoping always to convey swift and violent action. The fight between Hercules and Antaeus was a favorite subject. According to the myth, Antaeus could not be defeated as long as he was able to gain strength from his mother, Earth. Hercules cleverly reasoned that he might win the struggle only if his opponent never touched the ground. The story offers a splendid challenge for an artist hoping to exhibit his knowledge of anatomy, and as we can see from Signorelli's drawing (Plate 16), the artist has succeeded in showing us every tension and stress of the fight. In the Pollaiuolos' *Martyrdom of Saint Sebastian* (Plate 17), naturalism has been entirely sacrificed to the desire to display a complete knowledge of anatomy and foreshortening. The two bowmen on the left are placed in the same position as those on the right, only front to back, so that we can see that the painter is able to realize each pose fully from every angle. The spiritual meaning of the exercise may have been lost in the process.

Landscape, too, interested the Renaissance artist. The Pollaiuolos paid particular attention to their backgrounds, and if we look behind the figures in *The Martyrdom of Saint Sebastian* we will see a splendid Tuscan landscape, with its gently rolling hills and dark cypress trees, unfold before our eyes. Mere linear perspective is not enough to give a true view of landscape. As objects recede from the eye their color changes and things seen very far in the distance take on a bluish tone. This is called *aerial perspective*. The Pollaiuolos had observed aerial perspective, but the small trees in the distance seem strangely clear.

One master of landscape in Renaissance painting was Andrea del Verrocchio (c. 1435–1488). Verrocchio, in *The Baptism of Christ* (Plate 18), bathes his distant views in mists so that things are seen uncertainly, as the eye would perceive them. These mists contribute to the holiness of the setting. He also favored the handsome silhouette of dark trees in the foreground. He, too, had a perfect grasp of anatomy. This is not surprising, as he is known, not as a painter, but as the greatest sculptor in Florence after the death of Donatello. His equestrian figure of Bartolommeo Col-

16. Luca Signorelli. *Hercules and Antaeus*, about 1490. *Windsor, England, Royal Collection.*

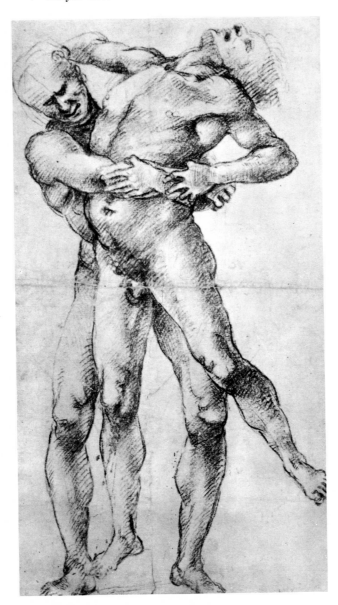

17. Antonio and Piero Pollaiuolo. *The Martyrdom of Saint Sebastian*, about 1475. *London, National Gallery.*

18. Andrea del Verrocchio. *The Baptism of Christ*, about 1470. *Florence, Uffizi Gallery.*

19. Andrea del Verrocchio. Monument to Bartolommeo Colleoni, about 1479–1490. *Venice.*

leoni (Plate 19), the *condottiere* who defeated Milan for the Venetians, is often compared with Donatello's *Il Gattamelata* (see Plate 9). When we examine them together, we can see that Donatello may have used classical statuary as his model, but Verrocchio almost certainly turned to a human model.

The new techniques and discoveries of Renaissance art soon spread to the other cities of Italy and were copied by their artists. In Mantua, Andrea Mantegna (*c.* 1431–1506) was so influenced by classical art that his painted figures are considered by some to look as if they are chiseled from stone, and certainly they give the monumental effect of Roman statuary. Mantegna was fascinated by perspective and the technique of foreshortening a figure, as *The Dead Christ* (Plate 20) suggests. It was he who developed the technique of painting a scene as if viewed from below — a technique called *di sotto in su* — which was later of great importance in the decoration of ceilings.

Meanwhile, Donatello had moved to Padua; Perugia could boast the master Perugino; and the d'Este family, the rulers of Ferrara, had become great patrons of art.

Venice clung for many years to her Byzantine traditions, although Donatello, Uccello, and Castagno all worked there. Gripped in the rule of the Senate and the Council of Ten under the yearly elected Doge, the city was as conservative in politics as in art. All citizens were to obey the few noble families who ruled, and there were to be no changes in Venice's institutions. Citizens, when abroad, were to spy for the state, and the crafts with which Venice traded, like glass blowing, were considered state secrets. Those citizens who disobeyed might be found floating in the canals, and drowned bodies were daily exhibited in the piazzas. But Venice had its lighter side, far lighter. If citizens were not permitted to interfere with the running of the state, they were very nearly *commanded* to enjoy themselves. There were endless fairs and festivals, and a good deal of Venetian art was concerned with portraying these pageants in the most precise detail and in the gorgeous colors for which the dyes of Venice were famous.

The Bellini family, into which Mantegna married, brought Renaissance techniques to Venice; the Bellinis were the finest painters of this splendid pageantry. They were, above all, masters of color. It was Giovanni Bellini (*c.* 1430–1516) who first used color to suggest the mood of a painting. In his *Pietà* (Plate 21) the grief at the suffering of Christ is expressed by the bleak, pale light shed by an obscured sun in a lead-gray sky.

It was in Venice, too, that a new medium first appeared in Italy — oil paint. Formerly, paintings had been executed in tempera, a medium in which the color pigment is mixed with raw egg and other ingredients. The

20. Andrea Mantegna. *The Dead Christ*, about 1506.
Milan, Brera Gallery.

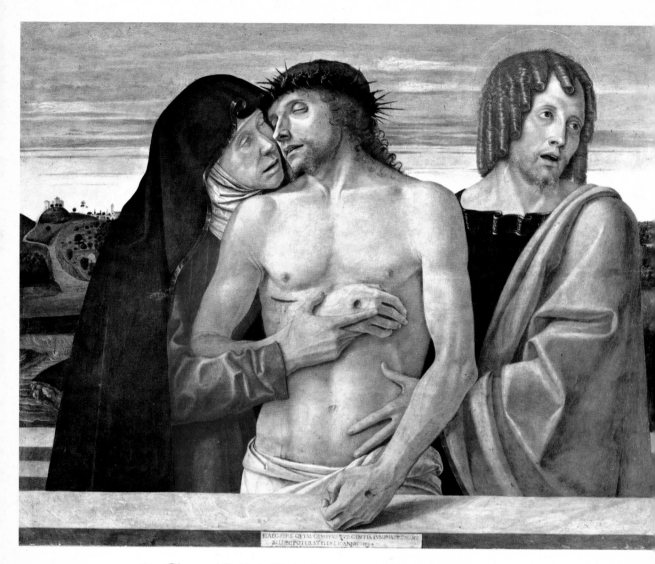

21. Giovanni Bellini. *Pietà*, about 1470. *Milan, Brera Gallery.*

new medium, whereby pigments are mixed with oil, was brought to Venice by the Sicilian painter Antonello da Messina (*c.* 1430–1479), but it was not an Italian invention. Oil painting was first used far to the north, in Flanders.

Flanders, the area containing portions of present-day Belgium and Holland, was enjoying its own Renaissance. Here, too, the cities were wealthy with trade and the textile industry, and the burghers dressed their wives in rich but sensible clothing, as expensive but not as showy as Italian wear, and they built themselves snug and upright mansions filled with comforts.

The Flemish Renaissance was very different from the Renaissance in Italy. Scholars might apply themselves to the study of Greek and Latin texts, but there were no splendid remains of architecture and statuary to inspire the artist, and study of the nude had little appeal in the chilly north. Rather, the artists of the north continued in the minutely detailed style of Gothic artists such as the Limbourg brothers; careful observation of detail led them to make the discoveries that Italian artists had arrived at by means of elaborate theories.

The earliest and greatest painters of this Flemish Renaissance were the van Eyck brothers, Hubert (*c.* 1366–1426) and Jan (1385–1441), painter to the court of Philip the Good, Duke of Burgundy, at Bruges. Jan van Eyck's *Madonna of Canon van der Paele* (Plate 22) is a truly extraordi-

22. Jan van Eyck. *The Madonna of Canon van der Paele*, 1436. *Bruges, Belgium, Musée Communal.*

nary work. The surface textures were so closely observed that we can almost feel the heavy velvets and wools, the canon's fine linen, the thick tapestry of the carpet, and the armor's dully burnished steel — all textures very dear to the merchants of Bruges. Van Eyck's perspective is perfect, not because he drew perspective lines and vanishing points, but because he observed so minutely the angles that he saw forming every object he painted. The same is true of color; he observed every tone so carefully that he achieved something never achieved before, even in Italy: he captured the effect of light and atmosphere — air, in fact — within the enclosure of a room. It is as if his figures, faintly Gothic in appearance and totally Gothic in spirit, inhabited a setting of photographic reality. The effect is almost alarming. But if we look from face to face, we see that these are not Gothic images at all, but people we might recognize on any street corner in the world.

This painting is extraordinary in yet another way — because of the Canon van der Paele himself. Owners and patrons who donated altarpieces had appeared, themselves, in these pieces before. But the Canon van der Paele not only kneels by the Virgin's side; he is the same size as she is. And so the good burghers of Flanders had grown in stature until they were not merely the equals of the noblemen, but occupied an important place in the presence of the Almighty.

Jan van Eyck perfected the art of oil painting as never before or since. His colors have not faded in five centuries, and later artists have tried in vain to discover the secret of how his paints were mixed. We must remember that fresco painting on the walls of churches and palaces would have quickly decayed in the damp of the north, and therefore artists like the van Eycks preferred to use wooden panels for altarpieces, while easel paintings came into fashion for private homes.

The van Eyck brothers were followed by a series of able painters including men like Roger van der Weyden (1399/1400–1464) who traveled back and forth to Italy and exchanged ideas and techniques with Italian painters. The *Portrait of Martin van Nieuwenhove* (Plate 23), by Hans Memling (about 1433–1494), the German-born artist who worked in Bruges, shows us how brilliantly the Flemish artists' technique of ob-

23. Hans Memling. *Portrait of Martin van Nieuwenhove*, 1487. *Bruges,
Belgium, Hospital of Saint John.*

serving details availed them in the field of portraiture. Italian artists, too, painted portraits of their patrons, but few could match the telling mirror-likenesses of the northern painters, whose models confront you, face to face today, in the galleries of Europe.

As we have seen, Jan van Eyck did his greatest work for the Duke of Burgundy. The artists of the Renaissance, both in Italy and in the north, owed as much to private individuals as to the Church, if not more. But who were these patrons? They might be landed nobility, like the Duke of Burgundy, or wealthy merchants, but in Italy they were usually the rulers of cities or towns. Democracy had in fact decayed in Italy during the fifteenth century. A wealthy family like the Medici bankers of Florence might come to power in the guilds and eventually, by dint of economic pressure, become virtual dictators of the city. Or, because of constant squabbles and petty wars, a *condottiere* with his own army might seize a town he was fighting or defending and turn it into a private dukedom. Or he might be rewarded for his success by falling heir to a principality. Francesco Sforza was such a *condottiere* — handsome, fearless, and eventually Duke of Milan.

These families were the great patrons of Italy: it was they who commissioned known artists and their workshops to decorate their palaces and the churches and public buildings they donated to the state. Contributions toward the construction of public buildings, they felt, were a duty that they owed to the honor of the family and of their ancestors. Their courts, all over Italy, became fevered centers of artistic activity. Family honor and an unquenchable thirst for public praise — these are what inspired many Renaissance patrons. Patronage was sensible politics as well. A ruler who gave the crowd splendid buildings for public use and enjoyment could count on loyalty in time of trouble. The public truly enjoyed art. The unveiling of a statue or a new series of frescoes would be attended by the entire town and would be the local topic of conversation for weeks. Everyone had the right to his opinion; art was for the many; it was not a special taste. It was a political weapon.

Federigo di Montefeltro, the Duke of Urbino, was the patron of Piero della Francesca. The d'Estes of Ferrara commissioned works by Mantegna, Jacopo Bellini, and Roger van der Weyden. But the greatest of all patrons of art were the Medici of Florence. Cosimo de' Medici, the founder of the family fortunes, was the patron of both Brunelleschi and Donatello, whom he supported through illness in his old age. Pollaiuolo and Verrocchio worked for the Medici, among many others, and Lorenzo de' Medici, called the Magnificent, was possibly the greatest patron of all time. When we say that Lorenzo was a great patron of the arts, however, we are not referring to painting and sculpture alone. He collected every type of material object of beauty or interest: antique statuary, manuscripts, objects of gold and silver. The Medici spent more on their collection of engraved gems than on sculpture and painting. Moreover, Cosimo de' Medici had recognized the importance of the philosophy of Plato and established an academy to study it. His grandson Lorenzo kept about him a circle of the great humanists of his day, men to whom the study of classical literature was considered the highest and sweetest pursuit in life. The painter Sandro Botticelli (1444/45–1510) was a member of the group.

This fact is extraordinary in itself, but the position of the artist had changed a great deal since Giotto's day. Then the painter had simply been a craftsman and a guild member, working in his workshop and accepting what commissions came his way. But to the Romans an artist had been as important as a poet; he was a creator and not merely a copier of nature. This is what Cicero thought, and the humanists accepted his judgment. Then too, in order to employ the kind of classical subject matter the humanists enjoyed in art, the artist would need a classical education. At the beginning of the fifteenth century the sculptor Ghiberti said that the artist should study grammar, geometry, philosophy, astrology, perspective, history, medicine, anatomy, arithmetic, and the theory of design. By the end of the century, a painter such as Botticelli might take his place among the intellectuals of his day.

Botticelli was altogether strange. He was not even a Renaissance artist as far as technique was concerned. He had little use for scientific perspective and even less for anatomy. His paintings were a symphony of rippling lines and he could almost have been a Gothic artist. And yet he was a Renaissance painter, and nothing less than a genius, in creating classical visions like *The Birth of Venus* (Plate 24). His Venus has remained the final type and symbol of feminine beauty to this day.

The dancing lines of the painting give a sense of the very breath of life. The sea may be a decorative design, the anatomy of the figures is far from perfect, but none of this matters. This artist is not re-creating reality, but something very different — sheer beauty. Venus is blown ashore by Zephyrus, god of the west wind, and is greeted by Chastity. But the symbolism of the painting has certain hidden Christian meanings as well.

24. Sandro Botticelli. *The Birth of Venus, 1486. Florence, Uffizi Gallery.*

In Lorenzo's circle the two philosophies, Christian and pagan, were part of one philosophy of life; without Plato, these people felt, it would be hard to be a good Christian and a good citizen.

Gradually subjects from classical mythology, commissioned by patrons such as the Medici, were taking their place beside the traditional religious topics commissioned by the Church or for it. But this does not mean that the artists of the Renaissance merely copied Greek and Roman art, any more than they copied Greek and Roman architecture. If we quickly compare the *Birth of Venus* with any work from ancient Rome, we can see immediately that they are literally worlds apart.

The figure of Chastity is dressed in the splendid patterned textiles for which Italy was famous, and in the fashion of Botticelli's time. The painters and sculptors of the Renaissance often interpreted scenes — biblical, historical, or classical — as happening in their own day, within settings of their own architecture and their own landscape — perhaps because it was the spirit that was important, and the spirit was eternal. We have seen this in Fra Angelico's *Annunciation*, Veneziano's *Madonna Enthroned*, Pollaiuolo's *Martyrdom of Saint Sebastian*, and even Uccello's *Saint George and the Dragon*. Certainly the artists of the Renaissance had a clear idea of classical dress and architecture, and yet Botticelli's is a Renaissance Venus. Again, it is the spirit that is important, and the mythical birth of Venus, like the struggle of Hercules and Antaeus, is only an occasion for creating a work that belonged entirely to the fifteenth century in spirit.

Many historians believe that the year 1500 marked the beginning of what we call modern civilization in Europe. There were momentous changes — changes that would alter man's whole way of life: the printing press, first invented in Germany in the mid-fifteenth century, was coming into use and Columbus had just discovered America. Moreover, there was a great spiritual upheaval in Europe. The humanism of the Medici, the concentration on worldly luxury, beauty, and material success in trade had gone too far. It had spread to the clergy, and many of the popes had a taste for what is called worldly pleasure. Some kept mistresses, some loved their food too well, and some collected antique works of art. The

Borgia Pope Leo X attempted to pass the papacy on to his illegitimate son Cesare, and Pope Alexander VI had an image of Venus inlaid in his emerald cross. All this extravagance was supported with money raised by questionable means such as the selling of indulgences, literally favors.

The people, suffering from constant wars and plagues, were in desperate need of some spiritual power to which they could turn. The first rumblings came in Florence, where the monk Savonarola harangued the population to drive out the Medici, who had robbed them of their power, and to abolish all the frivolous notions of the humanists with them. Savonarola raised a 70-foot "Bonfire of Vanities" and exhorted the people to throw into it all the momentos of their ungodly lives. Wigs, rouge boxes, dice — all went up in flame along with classical works of art. Unfortunately, one artist heard too well. Botticelli became so smitten with guilt at the monk's fiery words that it is said he threw his works on the flames and became what was called a *piagnone*, a "sniveling" follower of the pious preacher.

But the people of Florence, who were, after all, pleasure-loving and beauty-loving at heart, tired of Savonarola soon enough, and he ended up at the stake, burned as a heretic for his attacks on the Church. North of the Alps, however, things were not so easily settled. The northerners were more dour, more dissatisfied. The glorious glow of humanism had never really warmed them, and the Pope in Rome had wrung money from them to provide himself with Italian luxuries they did not appreciate. They took a grim view of human character; we see it reflected in the nightmare fantasies of Hieronymus Bosch (*c.* 1450–1516). Life was a *Ship of Fools* (Plate 25) on which people who were the very soul, the personification, of greed, selfishness, jealousy, and every vice, embarked toward eternity. A drunken priest is a prominent figure in the boat, while the Devil rides the mast. In 1517, the inevitable happened. Martin Luther posted his criticisms of the Church of Rome on the door of Wittenberg Cathedral, and northern Europe began its break with Catholicism.

The early sixteenth century was a confused nightmare of barbarism and wars in Italy. Charles VIII of France had read too many romances and tales of chivalry and wanted to rule the Kingdom of Naples; Louis XII

25. Hieronymus Bosch. *The Ship of Fools*, after 1500.
     Paris, Louvre.

of France had a hereditary claim to Milan; the Emperor Charles V, ruler of both Spain and the Holy Roman Empire, wanted to unite all Europe under his power. His motto was "Toujours plus outre" (Ever onward), and in his efforts he came face to face with François I of France, a fearless and iron-fisted monarch, the first Frenchman of the Renaissance, whose lionlike head and huge nose, as depicted by Jean Clouet (Plate 26) and others, can be recognized by every art student. Charles and François fought a life-and-death struggle for the fate of Europe, and Italy was their battleground. The towns and cities were at one moment wooed with promises, at another moment pillaged and burned.

Nothing was certain. Florence had enough problems of her own. She fought Pisa. The Medici were thrown out, then restored. Flanders captured the cloth trade and the Medici bank went into decline. It was hardly the moment for a great epoch in art. Yet Italy, in the early sixteenth century, saw the greatest era in the entire history of art, the **High Renaissance**.

When we think of the High Renaissance we think of three masters so brilliant that their names alone represent great art: Leonardo da Vinci (1452–1519), Michelangelo Buonarroti (1475–1564), and Raphael, or Raffaello, Sanzio (1483–1520). For these men the problems of technique, of anatomy and perspective, of light, were all solved. Every discovery of the fifteenth century was easily put to use, almost as second nature. More than any of the masters who preceded them, the artists of the High Renaissance were able to use technique effortlessly to interpret the world and create images of beauty.

Raphael was the youngest of the three, the least complicated. He was the best-loved painter of his time: "Raphael was so gentle and so charitable that even animals loved him, not to speak of men," said Vasari. Other artists loved him, his assistants loved him, and his many patrons loved him. Although he received his training in the north, Raphael, like Michelangelo, executed his finest works for the greatest patron of his time, Pope Julius II, in Rome. Raphael's technique was sure (Plate 27); he learned his anatomy, as best he could, from Michelangelo, and his shading from Leonardo. Raphael's creations had the grand breadth, the muscular might, and

26. Jean Clouet. *François I,*
first half sixteenth century.
Paris, Louvre.

27. Raphael. *Study of Two Apostles,* about 1517.
Oxford, England, Ashmolean Museum.

the freedom of movement of the High Renaissance. The sometimes
wooden puppetlike figures of a century before seem millennia away.

Raphael was known for his Madonnas. He created the image of the
sweet and loving Madonna and the human and playful Christ child that
was to inspire faith for four centuries. *The Madonna of the Goldfinch*
(Plate 28) is a good example. The flesh tones are imperceptibly shaded
and immensely touchable. The finish is perfect. The composition is a tri-
angle of superb grace, as the Madonna caresses Saint John, who holds the

28. Raphael. *The Madonna of the Goldfinch*, about 1506. *Florence, Uffizi Gallery.*

tiny bird for the infant Christ. The setting is one of total peace. Blue hills melt into a golden afternoon sun; not a breath of air rustles the trees — it is the peace of God. But where are the torture, bloodshed, and anguish of the year 1506? We can find them in the work of Michelangelo Buonarroti.

If Lorenzo de' Medici had done nothing else, his assistance in the education of Michelangelo would have been enough. He invited the young sculptor of good but impoverished family to study the antique works filling his garden and treated him like a son. Michelangelo, then, was a young member of Lorenzo's enchanted circle of humanists, although he was blunt in speech and stingy in his habits and always lacked the humanists' personal polish. But he grasped their philosophy and it became the core of his work.

Man was all, and Michelangelo's sole interest was the human figure. He studied antique statuary and human models; he dissected corpses. In portraying the body of man he surpassed not only Donatello and Verrocchio, but possibly even Phidias himself. Drapery and elaborate perspective settings did not interest him. He created such muscular figures of energy and power as had not been seen before, nor have they since. In the words of Bernard Berenson in *The Italian Painters of the Renaissance*, "Michelangelo completed what Masaccio had begun, the creation of the type of man best fitted to subdue and control the earth, and who knows! perhaps more than the earth."

Michelangelo's *The Creation of Adam* and *Moses* (Plates 29 and 30) are both such figures. Adam has just received the spark of life, but even though he is relaxed and just awakening, we see that he possesses the entire force of the human race. Moses is even more arresting. His energy expresses the power of the lawgiver, of the triumph of good over evil. Both were created for Pope Julius II, the great patron of the High Renaissance.

The Creation of Adam is part of the vast fresco painted for the Sistine Chapel in Rome. Michelangelo always considered himself a sculptor. The commission to paint this huge ceiling, working at a height of more than 60 feet on a surface always over his head, gave him no pleasure. Yet in the space of three years he completed 343 figures telling the entire story

of the Creation from the Beginning until Noah. At the ceiling's unveiling, the crowd was so large and caused such a commotion that the dust that was raised can be seen to this day.

The figure of Moses was sculpted for the Tomb of Julius II. This was another monumental project that the Pope himself commissioned during

30. Michelangelo. *Moses:* from the Tomb of Julius II, about 1515. *Rome, San Pietro in Vincoli.*

his lifetime. But Michelangelo was constantly fighting with his patron, and at one point an argument over the purchase of marble led him to walk out and return to his native Florence. The Pope demanded his return to Rome, but the Florentines insisted that Michelangelo stay. The Pope menaced, but the Florentines stood firm. War was threatened — over an artist.

In 1520, Michelangelo was asked to design the Medici Chapel in the Church of San Lorenzo in Florence. It was to be the burial place of two lesser-known members of the Medici family. In Plate 31 we see Guiliano de' Medici's tomb. Michelangelo created the setting as well as the sculpture, and the grand and ample proportions of this architecture are far nearer to those of ancient Rome than to the thinner and more confined, more "Gothic," designs of the early Renaissance. The figure of the duke himself is not a portrait. Michelangelo's attitude toward portraiture was casual: "In a thousand, nay a hundred years, no one will know or care who they are." What we see here is a handsome figure of alert strength. According to Vasari, Michelangelo "hated to imitate a living person if it were not someone exceedingly beautiful."

Giuliano seems about to spring into action, but exactly why remains a mystery. So does the meaning of the two strange figures on the sarcophagus, the coffin itself. On the left is a female figure slumped into a despairing sleep, her powerful body tortured by a nightmare. The figure on the right seems to awaken, not to the pleasure of light but to some disastrous dawn. His head hardly emerges from the stone. But extreme realism is no longer important. These are not merely characters enacting a part in a biblical drama; their role does not have to be defined. Michelangelo used the nude human body to express every sentiment, every abstract idea, the anguish of a struggling civilization itself. The figures have been called Night and Day, and Michelangelo wrote of his sleeping woman:

> Sweet is my sleep, but more to be mere stone,
> So long as ruin and dishonor reign,
> To bear nought, to feel nought, is my great gain;
> Then wake me not, speak in an undertone

Michelangelo set to work on the Medici Chapel in 1526. In 1527, the

31. Michelangelo. The Tomb of Guiliano de' Medici (detail), 1526–1531.
Florence, San Lorenzo, Medici Chapel.

German Imperial Army of Charles V, roaming the countryside, sacked Rome with a barbarity that left Italy stunned. The population was massacred, tortured, or sold into slavery. Churches were burned to the ground, works of art were destroyed or stolen, and the cardinals and the Pope were very nearly murdered.

But, as we have seen, the true spirit of the Renaissance was to be found in a certain scientific turn of mind, especially among artists. It is not surprising, then, that the greatest scientific mind of the age, the greatest in the history of man until only very recently, should have belonged to a man who may also have been the greatest painter of all time, Leonardo da Vinci.

Michelangelo was an architect as well as a painter, sculptor, and poet. During the Renaissance a man of learning was expected to be accomplished in many fields — this was especially true of artists. Brunelleschi was an archaeologist and an expert at engineering and optics as well as a sculptor in bronze, wood, gold, and silver; and the workshop of the Pollaiuolos produced sculpture, gold work, engravings, and even designs for tapestries. The young Leonardo, son of a notary, and a student of Verrocchio, was also a talented musician and mathematician, but this was far from enough. The artists of the century before had analyzed visual reality, finding laws for the way things looked. Leonardo went further. He wanted to see beneath the surface, to learn how they functioned.

Today the idea that any one person can possess all knowledge seems absurd. But during the Renaissance, when so much less was known, it still seemed possible, and this is what Leonardo wished to do. He kept careful records of his observations, experiments, and discoveries in his now famous notebooks — five thousand pages of carefully illustrated notes, closely written from right to left so that they could not be read unless held up to a mirror. He wrote not only on painting and sculpture, but on anatomy, aeronautics, geology, physical geography, the atmosphere, water and the building of canals, movement and weight in physics, mathematics, botany, optics, acoustics, and astronomy.

> The solar rays . . . take a straight and continuous course to the ground . . . [the moon] has greater colds and greater heats, and

its equinoxes are colder than ours ... the stars are visible by
night and not by day, owing to our being beneath a dense
atmosphere ... the earth from off the slopes and the lofty sum-
mits of the mountains has already descended to their bases, and
has raised the floors of the seas. . . . Where flame cannot live,
no animal that draws breath can live.

Intricately drawn illustrations — the cross section of a leaf, the human
embryo, patterns of clouds and water — make his statements clearly com-
prehensible. These may be facts that we learn at school, but Leonardo
gathered them from his own observations; it was one of the great feats
of the human mind. The conclusions at which he arrived were uncanny:
his study of fossils proved to his satisfaction that the earth was once covered with water.

Leonardo's observations led to an extraordinary number of inventions:
a kind of parachute and a helicopter, inflatable lifesavers, a hydrophonic
device for communication between ships, a mechanical excavator, roller
bearings, the rolling mill, a device for measuring the speed of wind — the
list is endless. And yet this extraordinary man signed his letters *Leonardus
Vincius, Pictor* — Leonardo da Vinci, Painter.

It was as a painter that Leonardo worked for Ludovico Sforza (called
Il Moro, "the dark one") in Milan. That such a man as Leonardo should
have left Florence to join the bloodiest tyrant in all Italy may amaze us,
but Leonardo was very different from the other humanists of Florence.
They looked to Latin texts for their information; Leonardo looked directly at nature. He did not even bother to learn Latin until he was at an
advanced age. "Whoever in discussion calls upon authority uses not his
intellect but rather his memory," he said. Ludovico was a man of action.
The members of his court were interested in mathematics and mechanics.
This was an atmosphere that pleased Leonardo. For the duke he painted
portraits and organized festivals. He even designed costumes — and weapons of war. Ludovico gave Leonardo the peace and leisure to pursue his
studies. When Louis XII and his French army seized Milan, the duke fled
and Leonardo began a life of wandering, working for one state, then another, until he died far away in France, a guest of François I. He saw
political problems as temporary; he did not take sides.

As a painter, too, Leonardo was an innovator. He was famous for his chiaroscuro, his use of light and shade. He discarded the sharp outlines of earlier painters, creating around his figures a misty atmosphere and depth. Let us look again at Verrocchio's *Baptism of Christ* (Plate 18). It is possible that the angel on the left and the landscape directly behind it were in fact painted by Verrochio's young pupil Leonardo. As we can see in Leonardo's drawing *The Virgin and Child with Saint Anne and Saint John the Baptist* (Plate 32), he created his compositions not with lines and patches of color, but with areas of light and shadow that blend into one another by fine gradation. This simple charcoal sketch tells us something else about Leonardo, something perhaps surprising. He was a deeply religious man and the gentle and shadowy atmosphere with which he surrounds his figures becomes one of holiness.

Unfortunately, Leonardo undertook few works and finished fewer still. Less than a dozen of his paintings survive and no sculpture at all. But the *Mona Lisa* (Plate 33), his portrait of the third wife of the Florentine merchant Bartolomeo del Giocondo, is perhaps the most famous of all paintings. It has been praised for the dreamy mists of its background and the infinitely delicate flesh tones of the figure. Its mysteries have been analyzed. One side of the mouth is curled into a smile and the other is not; the eyes do not match; one side of the background is higher than the other. But it is some other quality that makes this picture great. It is the expression of the Mona Lisa herself. She looks out at us as if she knows us and as if she knows life. Like her creator (Plate 34), she seems to be the possessor of all knowledge.

During the High Renaissance, Venice produced painters of her own. Venice was the "jewel casket of the world." She traded in spices, silks and damasks, mosaic work, lace, bronzes, armor, slaves, and printed books. But the Venetians did not *write* books. Venice could boast scarcely a single author or philosopher, scientist or scholar. She could not provide the atmosphere for serious thought. It was said that Venetian women would not appear in public unless wearing jewels and trimmings worth at least five thousand ducats, that they wore their dresses so low they almost fell off, that they bleached their hair, and that they painted every part of

32. Leonardo da Vinci. *The Virgin and Child with Saint Anne and Saint John the Baptist*, about 1501. *London, National Gallery.*

33. Leonardo da Vinci. *Mona Lisa*, about 1504. *Paris, Louvre.*

34. Leonardo da Vinci. *Self-portrait*, about 1512. *Turin, Italy,
    Biblioteca Reale.*

35. Titian. *Sacred and Profane Love* (detail), about 1515.
   Rome, Borghese Gallery.

their face, even their teeth. The Venetians loved every visual beauty, and above all, they loved fine easel paintings. The artists of Venice returned their affection. They loved the beauty of Venice, the jewels and rich silks, the dark-eyed courtesans with their hair bleached blond by the sun. This was often what they painted, no matter what the subject was meant to be.

Titian (*c.* 1487/90–1576), the greatest of the Venetian masters, chose a courtesan as the model for his painting *Sacred and Profane Love* (Plate 35). He was famous for the golden hair and melting flesh tones of the women in his paintings, for his superb use of oil paint, built up with glaze upon glaze of color, and for his penetrating portraits. In a material way he was, in fact, the most successful painter who ever lived. He was more important than the Doge; the great men of his day came to visit his splendid palace in Venice. He was a friend of the Emperor Charles V, and a true Venetian, dealing in corn and wood on the side.

The Martyrdom of Saint Justina (Plate 36) by Paolo Veronese (1528–1588) is in the true Venetian spirit, a splendid decoration, a portrayal of sumptuous court life, with all the touchable textures of luxury — silks fine armor, furs, and horseflesh. That it is a dramatic scene of martyrdom might well be forgotten. Yet the painters of Venice could always capture the clever, calculating lively glance of its citizens, as in this portrait (Plate 37) by Jacopo Robusti, known as Tintoretto (1518–94). They were great portraitists and they understood all things Venetian.

The Venetians might well enjoy their wealth; it could not last. Times were changing. America and new routes to the East had already been discovered and soon they would destroy Venice's trade and so her legendary wealth. Meanwhile, the Church in Rome was losing its grip on the North, as one after another of the principalities of which Germany then consisted accepted the Protestant reforms, not without bloodshed. Meanwhile, Protestantism spread to the Netherlands, Sweden, and Denmark, and in England, Henry VIII, desiring the freedom of divorce, established

36. Paolo Veronese. *The Martyrdom of Saint Justina* (detail), about 1575. *Padua, Italy, Museo Civico.*

37. Tintoretto. *Portrait of Vincenzo Morosini*, about 1580–1585.
London, National Gallery.

himself as head of the Church of England. France was torn by the bloody Wars of Religion. Everywhere church property was seized and works of art destroyed. The new religion had no use for graven images, for any of the lighter indulgences of life. In Geneva, the stronghold of the reformer John Calvin, there was to be no luxury, dancing, theater, games, or festivals. Long banquets, the breach of a promise of marriage, wearing two rings on one finger — all were crimes. Houses of worship were sparsely decorated and for all intents and purposes religious painting ceased to exist in Protestant Europe.

Still, two of the greatest painters of the sixteenth century were northerners, artists of the hectic period of change. The Reformation caught Hans Holbein the Younger (1497/98–1543) in mid-career. As a young man, he had painted religious scenes of almost alarming realism — the detailed realism of the northern artists, although he traveled in Italy and absorbed the grander style of Leonardo. But when his work in painting the Council Chamber in Basel was interrupted by the disturbances of the Reformation, he decided to leave the Continent and settle in England. He was already known as a superb portraitist, and portraiture was a form of art accepted by the Protestants (Plate 38). Holbein painted Luther himself. In England, his style — the hard-edged, almost shadowless portraits conveying a likeness so real it was almost alarming — had great success. Remaining there for most of the rest of his life, he eventually became court painter to Henry VIII. The great Dutch humanist Erasmus; Sir Thomas More (Plate 39), who refused to grant the king's desire for a divorce and lost his head on the block; the Duke of Norfolk, who sentenced his own niece Anne Boleyn to death — all the personages in the strange and tortured pages of history that were the reign of Henry VIII were known to Holbein and were painted by him. And so it is that we have a clearer notion of the actors in this long and bloody drama than we have of any other group of people in history until the invention of the camera. But Holbein tells us what no camera can. Like all great portraitists, he could see into the very souls of his subjects — the robust, pigheaded Henry (Plate 40) and the crafty, small-minded Norfolk alike.

But it was Albrecht Dürer (1471–1528) who brought the theories, the

38. Hans Holbein the Younger. *Burgomaster Jakob Meyer*, 1516. *Basel, Switzerland, Kunstmuseum.*

39. Hans Holbein the Younger.
    Portrait of Sir Thomas More,
    1527. *New York,*
    Frick Collection.

40. Hans Holbein the Younger.
    Portrait of Henry VIII (detail),
    about 1530. *Lugano, Switzerland,*
    Thyssen Collection.

"scientific" art of Renaissance Italy, to the north. Despite the northern artists' close observation and knowledge of how to paint surface textures, the Gothic spirit was still strong among them. As a young man, Dürer visited Italy and studied the works of Mantegna and Pollaiuolo. He wanted to learn the rules, the theories of perspective and anatomy and perfect beauty — matters that had not previously concerned the northern artists. He was a master engraver, and he drew the nude again and again, until in paintings and engravings like his *Adam and Eve* (Plate 41) he was able to capture the muscular perfection and sense of solid bulk of the Italian artists. More than this, he did something that must have been extremely difficult: he brought this new knowledge to subjects completely northern and still Gothic in spirit. The results were engravings of tremendous religious power, such as *The Four Riders of the Apocalypse* (Plate 42). The entire composition is a rage of the delicate whirling line that delighted Gothic artists. Yet the horsemen and their mounts are splendid Renaissance figures and we can almost hear the poundings of the horses' hooves as they trample the sinful, a king and a priest among them. The

41. Albrecht Dürer. *Adam and Eve*, 1504. *London, British Museum.*

42. Albrecht Dürer. *The Four Riders of the Apocalypse:* from
The Apocalypse, 1498. *London, British Museum.*

43. Albrecht Dürer. *Self-portrait in a Fur Coat*, 1500. Munich, Germany, *Alte Pinakothek*.

picture is full of Gothic symbolism: the scales, the gaunt figure of Death, the angel above. It is an exciting, terrifying work.

Dürer's self-portrait (Plate 43) shows us that he understood the chiaroscuro, the light and deep shadows of Leonardo. It shows us, too, the face of the first Renaissance man of the north. Dürer had the active mind of Leonardo and the Renaissance men before him. He was a mathematician as well as an artist and he had a devouring curiosity about the natural world. He died of the lingering effects of a fever caught in a Zeeland swamp, where he had gone to examine at first hand the body of a whale.

IV

SPAIN and the NETHERLANDS

The Sixteenth and Seventeenth Centuries

DESPITE THE CONFUSION and bloodshed of the sixteenth century, the Europe we know today was taking shape. Books were printed and made available for the growing number of people who could read them. Leonardo was not the only man of science. Zoology came into being and a *History of Animals* was written by Konrad von Gesner (1516–1565). Mineralogy became a science, and zinc, bismuth, and arsenic were discovered. Vesalius (1514–1564) mapped out the human body, and the great Frenchman Ambroise Paré (1517–1590) revolutionized the practice of surgery. Copernicus (1473–1543), a Polish monk, proved that the earth turned around the sun. The Church, of course, objected. Vesalius was accused of opening the heart of a living man and was condemned to death. His sentence was commuted to the penance of a pilgrimage to the Holy Land, one sure way of disposing of him for a number of years. He drowned on the return voyage.

Meanwhile, habits were changing. New foods came from the New

World: maize and potatoes and many others, along with exotic plumage for hats and fans, rubber, coffee, and smoking tobacco. But most important, gold and silver stolen from the Indians of South America or dug out of the mines of the New World flowed into the coffers of the nations whose explorers — desperate, shrewd, brave, and ruthless men — literally seized the riches with their bare hands. The gold was spent on luxuries and was so disbursed that merchants and craftsmen were more prosperous than ever before. Meanwhile, the mental attitude of the Renaissance was spreading throughout Europe.

> To be, or not to be, that is the question —
> Whether 'tis nobler in the mind, to suffer
> The slings and arrows of outrageous fortune,
> Or to take arms against a sea of troubles,
> And, by opposing, end them? To die — to sleep —
> No more; . . .

These words, of the Danish Prince Hamlet in the play by the English poet William Shakespeare (1564–1616), were written in 1601, but they are the thoughts of a modern man. Is it better to suffer or to destroy oneself? There is no reference to some set medieval notion of punishment in Heaven or Hell. Prince Hamlet simply does not know and has not the courage to find out, but he wonders. And so the Renaissance had come to England with a series of brilliant writers: Edmund Spenser (*c.* 1552–1599) wrote his *Faerie Queene*, Sir Philip Sidney (1554–1586) his *Arcadia*, and Christopher Marlowe (1564–1593) and Shakespeare their plays, all in homage to Elizabeth I, who brought England into the Renaissance and made her a power to be reckoned with in Europe.

Bony, pale, and redheaded, Elizabeth came to the throne at the age of twenty-five amid a confusion of plots and counterplots. She was domineering and suspicious, as she had to be, but she was also the wisest ruler in England's history. She chose brilliant advisers: Walsingham, Bacon, and William Cecil. She preferred diplomacy to war, and she assisted the prosperity of the country in a hundred ways: a Poor Law to combat poverty, the founding of companies to exploit foreign markets, the welcoming of Flemish refugees skilled in the production of cloth, the reorganization of the fleet, even a three-day meatless fast to encourage the sale of fish. All these moves resulted in making England wealthier and more civilized than ever before. The nobility left their castles to live in gracious country houses built in a form of Gothic architecture, called Tudor, which is still popular in England. Merchants in the growing towns enjoyed all the comforts of carpets and feather beds. It is small surprise that Spenser saw his gawky and sallow monarch as a "Faerie Queene."

Elizabeth was a person of brilliant education who was fluent in Latin, Greek, and most European tongues. Above all, she loved the theater, poetry (which she composed herself), and music. Her courtiers were expected to be able to write verses and sight-read for impromptu musicales. And she prided herself on her dancing. Evenings at her court were whiled away in constant pageants, masques, and balls.

But to the visual arts of painting and sculpture, Elizabeth was quite blind. There were, of course, portrait painters in the never-forgotten tradition of Holbein, but the queen had some strange notions. She had no use for the chiaroscuro of a Leonardo. Shadows, she pronounced, looked like smudges on the face. Her favorite painter, Nicholas Hilliard (1537– 1619) wrote that portrait painting was "best in plaine lines without shadowing, for the lyne without shadow showeth all to a good judgment, but the shadow without line showeth nothing." And so the queen appears (Plate 1) elaborately jeweled and dressed in the huge sleeves and tight, pointed bodice of the day (she was very proud of her figure), with her white skin (of which she was also very proud) quite unshadowed. But art did not progress.

Elizabeth championed the cause of Protestantism in Europe. Her greatest triumph was the defeat of the Armada, the fleet of her deadliest enemy, Catholic Spain. But it was Spain, as backward in thought as England was advanced, that produced some of the greatest art of the age.

The Moors who had ruled Spain for centuries were driven out, once and for all, after their final defeat at the hands of the most Catholic king and queen, Ferdinand and Isabella, in that fateful year of 1492 — fateful too because Columbus's discovery of America launched the country on a career of empire building that brought a vast wealth of gold into her trea-

1. Nicholas Hilliard. *Queen Elizabeth*, about 1584. *London, British Museum.*

sury. Spain profited more than any nation in Europe from the wealth of America, and the riches went, not to develop Spain's industries, but to support her huge and greedy aristocracy and to administer her possessions in Europe and America. When Philip II, son of Charles V, came to the throne of Spain in 1556, he ruled the Netherlands, the Franche-Comté — a region in eastern France — a large part of Italy, and vast stretches of Central and South America.

But the Spaniards of the sixteenth century were grim, proud, joyless, and passionately religious. Philip himself, although a diligent and conscientious worker, ruled as a despot, relying on spies and informers. He never laughed. A chapel was built in his bedroom so that he could see the Sacrament from his bed, and before his death he commanded that a skull wearing a golden crown be put beside him — such was his temperament. The taste for black in clothing, which became popular throughout Europe in the sixteenth century, was a Spanish fashion. Still, it was an age of ridiculous luxury. In Portugal there were twice as many perfumers as teachers.

The Catholic Church was even more powerful in Spain than in Italy. But it was no longer the loose, pleasure-loving, immoral organization of the Renaissance popes. The reaction to the Protestant Reformation had been a violent one. With the Council of Trent (1545–1563) the Church reformed itself. In this Counter-Reformation, abuses were abolished and a true spirit of religious piety returned. But woe to the heretic. In order to stamp out Protestantism in the countries remaining Catholic, the deadly Inquisition was established — a high court with absolute authority to investigate, torture, and put to death anyone suspected of harboring "heretical" ideas. Nowhere was the Inquisition more active than in Spain. Within ten years, not a Protestant was left in the country. But it was not the Protestants against whom the Inquisition was aimed. Its real object was the conversion to Catholicism of the descendants of the Moors and of the Jews who had come to Spain with them. In this the Church and the king were relentless, making splendid public spectacles of the burning of hundreds of victims at a time. The Moors were forbidden to speak Arabic, wear the veil, or conduct their marriage and funeral ceremonies. Even Turkish baths were abolished. All traces of Moorish life were stamped out. In the New World, the same Inquisition was used to convert the "heathen" Indians. The dark side of the Spanish character thrived on such grisly entertainments.

The Counter-Reformation bred a new kind of art in Italy, as well. What might have been lacking in true faith was replaced with exaggerated emotion by the sculptors, the painters, and even the architects of the Baroque style. Everything about Baroque art was exaggerated. Baroque statuary such as *Ecstasy of Saint Theresa* (Plate 2), by Giovanni Lorenzo Bernini (1598–1680), wafted heavenward with sheer ecstatic emotion. In painting, artists such as Caravaggio (1573–1610) used the shock effects of extravagant gestures and lighting to give their canvases all the drama of theatrical performances (Plate 3).

2. Giovanni Lorenzo Bernini. *Ecstasy of Saint Theresa*, 1645–1652. *Rome, Santa Maria della Vittoria.*

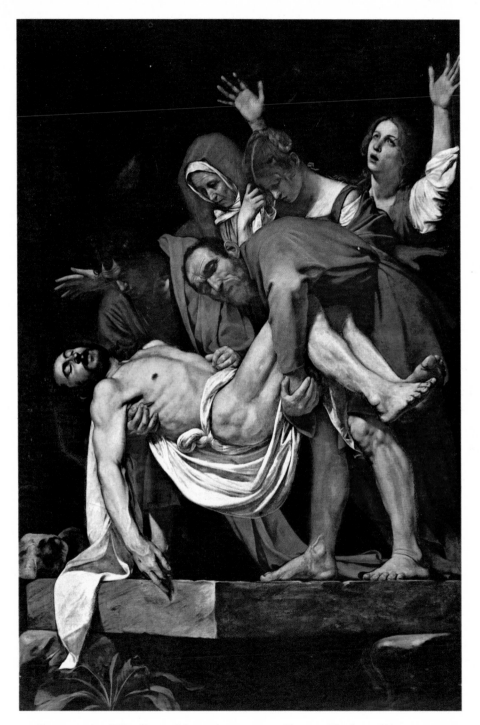

3. Caravaggio. *The Deposition*, about 1604. *Rome, Vatican, Pinacoteca*.

Spanish Christian art was Gothic until the end of the sixteenth century, with a special love for polychrome, or "many-colored," wooden statues. The Renaissance was slow in coming and when it came it was in the form of the resplendent, elaborate, exaggerated Baroque. We must remember that the Moors had left behind them intricately designed palaces and this elaborate decoration was to the Spanish taste.

But Spain of the sixteenth century might not have had great art had it not been for the chance arrival of an extraordinary artist, Domenikos Theotokopoulos (*c.* 1541–1614), born on the island of Crete and called by the Spaniards El Greco, "the Greek." El Greco had studied art in Venice, and why he chose to settle in backward Spain remains a mystery to this day. But in Spain he developed a style unlike any seen in the sixteenth century or any other.

The Burial of Count Orgaz (Plate 4) is one of El Greco's most famous works. In the lower part of the painting, we see the dour courtiers of Spain in their traditional black dress, their soulful, dark-eyed faces set off against their stiff white ruffs — another Spanish fashion. But above, the vision of the Heavenly Host greeting the count's spirit is not quite like anything we have seen before. El Greco put to use the dramatic lighting and extravagant gestures of the Baroque painters, but he went even further. He elongated his forms until the bounds of reality are broken altogether, his figures bursting into the tortured poses with which he was able to express the religious ecstasy of Spain herself. The colors, too, are strange. El Greco hated the sun, and his are the "colors of the moon": acid and clashing greens and yellows, amethyst pinks, and brilliant mauves and blues.

Perhaps even stranger than El Greco's art is the fact that it was not only accepted but was successful in Spain. It was not to everyone's liking, and the king himself admitted that he did not understand it. But a small group of noblemen admired El Greco and patronized him. One cannot help wondering what freedom of mind, in such an unfree country, prompted them to appreciate the first artist to abandon visual reality, to exaggerate and distort it, in order to achieve some higher reality, much as the artist does today.

4. El Greco. *The Burial of Count Orgaz*, 1586–1588. *Toledo, Spain, Saint Tomé.*

Spain was already in decline by the beginning of the seventeenth century. Rich with the vast hoard of gold from the Americas, the Spaniards had neglected their own industries and now they suffered. The country was bankrupt, plague-ridden, and depopulated. Grazing sheep impoverished the soil. Still, Spain was powerful, and for the next hundred years the Spanish court went blindly on its way entertaining itself with festivals and bullfights, spending money it did not have in waging wars it could not afford, to hold on to an empire that was slipping away. Spain was becoming a country of "shepherds, monks, and unemployed soldiers."

Still, this was the Golden Age of Spanish literature, when Lope de Vega wrote more than fifteen hundred plays, and Cervantes wrote about Don Quixote, a knight of the Middle Ages as blind as the Spanish court to the realities of the seventeenth century. It was the Golden Age of Spanish art as well, and the masters of the period put on their canvases both the religious passion of their country and the weak faces of their rulers, elaborately dressed but decaying from within.

José de Ribera (1591–1652), who settled in Italy, and Francisco de Zurbarán (1598–1664) were both artists of religious zeal. They were also Baroque painters, devoted to the dramatic lighting of Caravaggio and to his realism. Caravaggio had no use for the idealization of a Leonardo or a Michelangelo. Beautiful faces did not interest him. Even for his most

5. José de Ribera. *Jacob's Dream,* 1639. *Madrid, Prado.*

6. José de Ribera. *Saint Agnes in Prison*, 1641. *Dresden, Germany, Gemäldegalerie.*

devout paintings he chose his models from the common people, and he was accused of using a woman of the street for his *Death of the Virgin*. So, in Ribera's painting *Jacob's Dream* (Plate 5), Jacob might be a Spanish peasant. Both Ribera and Zurbarán were masters of the grace of saints

7. Diego Velázquez. *The Topers*, 1628. *Madrid, Prado.*

and the tortured death of martyrs (Plate 6), both very much to the Spanish taste.

But the true master of the age was Diego Velázquez (1599–1600). Velázquez, too, began by painting religious scenes, but these were not really his style. He soon became known for a new kind of picture — scenes from everyday life, or *genre* paintings. The Spaniards called such paintings *bodegones*, from the word meaning "eating house," because they often featured scenes of eating and drinking. Velázquez's painting *The Topers* (Plate 7) is an imaginative piece. A party of vagrants, all too fond of their drink — as we can see from their unshaven appearance and glazed eyes — are joined by Bacchi, mythical creatures crowned with vine leaves and personifying the spirit of wine. When asked why he painted such a subject, Velázquez said, "I would rather be first in this coarse stuff than second in nicety."

But Velázquez was a master of nicety as well. The Netherlands had long been part of the Spanish empire and, like the northern painters, Velázquez was a master at capturing the surface texture of things — so great a master that, like Jan van Eyck, he could "paint the air" within a room. And so, in *The Maids of Honor* (Plate 8), we see the artist at work

8. Diego Velázquez. *The Maids of Honor*, about 1656. *Madrid, Prado.*

in a chamber of the Alcazar Palace in Madrid. He must have been painting the royal couple when the little Infanta (Princess) Dona Margarita
came in with her maids of honor, her pet dog, and two of the dwarfs who
entertained the Spanish court. The Infanta appears like a small adult in the
wide, heavy, and uncomfortable fashion of the Spanish aristocrat — a
dress stiff with silver cloth. The picture is a trick. The artist has shifted
his point of view so as to capture himself at work and his true models, the
king and queen — reflected in the mirror at the back — while making the
subject of the picture the little Infanta and her train. So natural are the
poses that they seem caught for eternity in a moment's activity. The trick
has worked. One is tempted to ask, "Where is the picture?"

Velázquez knew his subjects well. He was appointed royal painter to
Philip IV in 1623, but he was also quartermaster general. In this post he
seems to have been responsible for everything. He arranged the meetings
of kings, the setting of the royal tables, and saw to it that guests in the
palace had chamber pots in their rooms. And so Velázquez lived daily
with his models, observing them at every turn, and all this he set down on
his canvases with a realism that was sometimes kind, but never flattering:
the gloomy Philip IV as his watery eyes and puffy face grew older, his
wife, Elizabeth of Bourbon; his appealing son, Balthasar Carlos; his second
wife, Mariana of Austria; and her daughter the Infanta Margarita. In his
paintings we see the growing gloom of the court as the king aged — his
only heir a retarded weakling who could not walk until the age of seven
— while his empire fell to pieces.

The northern part of the Netherlands was already long lost to Spain.
During the sixteenth century, Protestantism had found fertile soil there,
and when Philip II sent the Duke of Alba to enforce the Inquisition and
stamp out the new religion, the entire Netherlands rose in revolt against
the hated Spanish domination. By the end of the century, independence
was won and what had been the United Netherlands became two separate
countries, with the ten Catholic provinces of Belgium in the south, and the
Protestant United Provinces of Holland in the north.

From both sections of the Netherlands came great works of art. *The
Adoration of the Magi* (Plate 9) is by Peter Paul Rubens (1577–1640) of

9. Peter Paul Rubens. *The Adoration of the Magi*, 1624. *Antwerp, Belgium, Musée Royal des Beaux-Arts.*

Antwerp, who was a painter to Infanta Isabella and Archduke Ferdinand of the Belgian court. *The Lady Governors of the Old Men's Home at Haarlem* (Plate 10) is the work of the Dutch master Franz Hals (*c*. 1580–1666). A glance will tell us the difference between the art of Catholic and Protestant Europe.

The Adoration of the Magi is a splendid decoration in the Italian Baroque fashion. Rubens studied the work of the Venetians and he outdoes them in the painting of rich silks, furs, and soft, pale flesh; he has a northerner's understanding of the painting of textures. Above all, his colors are rich and brilliant in the true Venetian tradition. His composition is free, monumental, robust, and tremendously imaginative. He could cover a huge space with any number of figures and yet create a perfect composition. And he has a seventeenth-century knowledge of reality. He knows how a North African sultan or a camel would look as well as he knows how to portray the cows in the manger. The entire scene is a riot of grandiose color.

10. Frans Hals. *The Lady Governors of the Old Men's Home at Haarlem,* *1664. Haarlem, Netherlands, Franz Hals Museum.*

Rubens's career exemplifies that of the successful court painter. Having served as a page in his childhood, he studied art and traveled in Italy. He was called back to Antwerp to see his dying mother and immediately became painter to the court. Blond and handsome, and famous for his charm and his ability to speak languages, he was a perfect courtier — so perfect in fact, so thoroughly likable, that he was entrusted with highly important diplomatic missions. On one such mission he was knighted by Charles I of England and received an honorary degree from Cambridge University. He was a scholar, an antiquarian, even a bit of a scientist — in short, a Renaissance man of the north. Most important, he was a superlative painter. Certainly his huge compositions were well suited to covering the walls of palaces throughout Catholic Europe. He kept a large workshop of assistants busy and created religious and mythological scenes of a scope and grandeur rarely equaled.

But the people of Protestant Holland would not cover the walls of their churches with paintings and they possessed no palaces. In short, they would have had no use for a Rubens. Nor did they have a taste for religious or mythological subjects. Their excellent seamanship and flourishing trade had brought them some return, and the merchants of the towns, who were in comfortable circumstances, wanted easel paintings for the walls of their modest homes. In these paintings they wanted to see what was most familiar to them — landscapes of the countryside they knew, familiar streets (Plate 11), or scenes of their favorite pastimes (Plate 12). Portraits were of course popular, and often the members of an organization would pose in a group, like the *Lady Governors of the Old Men's Home in Haarlem*. And what a group we have here. Some kindly, others stern, all capable, and each one a distinct, recognizable character, primly seated in her brisk starched collar and coif. The hands alone, gnarled with a lifetime of work and care, tell us volumes. These are not the smooth hands of the richly dressed duchesses of Italy.

Not all such paintings are so very dour. The Dutch were particularly known for the hilarity of their scenes of tavern and home life (Plate 13). A woman drinking a bit more heartily than she should, a child stealing a puff from a pipe, a good deal of music and even more laughter — these

11. Pieter Saenredam. *The Square at Haarlem*, 1629. *The Hague,
    Netherlands, Koninklijke Bibliotheek.*

12. Jan van Goyen. *Winter Games near Leiden*, 1653. *Amsterdam,
    Rijksmuseum.*

13. Jan Steen. *The Artist's Family*, seventeenth century. *The Hague, Netherlands, Mauritshuis.*

were precisely the subjects that the Dutch loved best.

They wanted simple scenes, the scenes of which life is made. In Plate 14 we see a cook at work in a kitchen. But this is a cook as painted by the greatest master at recapturing visual, almost photographic, reality in the entire history of art — Jan Vermeer (1632–1675). Vermeer painted surface textures, light, and space so well that it is hard to believe we are looking at the flat surface of a painting, that we cannot rub our fingers over the rough seeds on the bread's crust or the chipped edge of the rim of the pitcher.

But one Dutch artist did not fit the pattern. He was Rembrandt van

14. Jan Vermeer. *Maid Pouring Milk*, 1658. *Amsterdam, Rijksmuseum.*

Rijn (1606–1669). Rembrandt began his career by giving his Dutch patrons exactly what they wanted — brilliantly executed portraits of themselves wearing the velvets and furs that were the mark of success, all meticulously painted. For these the young artist was amply rewarded and he bought himself a splendid house in Amsterdam and purchased clothing for his family and furniture so luxurious that he was criticized.

Then, in 1640, the clouds began to gather around Rembrandt's life. His wife died, as had all his children except one, a son named Titus. Moreover, his popularity as a portrait painter was declining, possibly because of his portrait of the militia company of Captain Franz Banning Cocq, a portrait called *The Night Watch* (Plate 15), in which he sacrificed individual portraits to the drama of the scene. In any case, he no longer cared. He turned now to painting and engraving religious subjects. That there was no demand for these did not matter. They were not decorations; there were no extravagant gestures to be seen from across a cathedral. There were inner visions of scenes from the Bible, painted to speak, soul to soul, to the individual viewer. Rembrandt went to the Ghetto, the

15. Rembrandt. *The Night Watch*, 1642. *Amsterdam, Rijksmuseum.*

poor Jewish quarter packed with refugees from the Spanish Inquisition. Here he found the faces that told, he felt, the true story of the Bible. He decked out his sorry models in the turbans and trappings of the Orient and painted them with a sympathy and understanding of human suffering never before put on a canvas. If we compare Rembrandt's *David Playing His Harp before Saul* (Plate 16) with Rubens's *Adoration of the Magi*, we can see how very far Rembrandt's works were from the sumptuous Baroque painting of his day. But Rembrandt's art is still deeply moving today, while Rubens's masterpiece seems a splendid piece of playacting. Rembrandt was, above all, the painter of the tragedy of human life, and this we see most clearly in his paintings of himself as, over the years, his illusions faded to an acceptance of fate. In Plate 17 we see his self-portrait painted when, bankrupt, living in poor lodgings, and almost totally alone, he saw with honesty the tragedy in his own worn features and brooding eyes and set this on canvas with a hand that was sure to the very end.

16. Rembrandt. *David Playing His Harp before Saul*, about 1657. *The Hague, Netherlands, Mauritshuis.*

17. Rembrandt. *Self-portrait*, 1658. *New York, Frick Collection.*

1. Hyacinthe Rigaud. *Portrait of Louis XIV. Paris, Louvre.*

V

FRANCE and ENGLAND
The Seventeenth and Eighteenth Centuries

As the power of Spain waned during the seventeenth century the power of France grew. France had been suffering more than a century of religious struggles and disorder when Louis XIV came to the throne in 1661 at the age of twenty-two. This extraordinary monarch brought order out of chaos and totally remolded the state.

As a young ruler, Louis was faced with one problem above all others — the power of the nobility. It is amazing how long feudalism had lasted in Europe. Not until the seventeenth century was it finally swept away and only then did centralized monarchy, the rule of the king alone, take possession of states throughout Europe. Louis accomplished this in a thoroughly original way. At home, in their well-fortified castles, surrounded by their peasants, the nobility were powerful. Therefore, he reasoned, they must remain at court where he could keep his eye on them. How was this to be achieved? Again, Louis struck on a masterful plan: in a thousand different ways he made his court fashionable, the only place to be.

To begin with, he set about constructing at Versailles near Paris the largest, most sumptuous palace ever built, designed to house ten thousand members of the court. Here life was conducted according to the most ironclad rules of etiquette, revolving around every action of the king. The most important members of the court were always to be on hand for his attendance at church services, for his meals, his rising in the morning, and his going to bed at night. On this last occasion some member of the court would be given the honor of carrying the royal candlestick. Then the Gentlemen of the Bedchamber and the Gentlemen of the Wardrobe — all members of the highest aristocracy — would remove his shoes, stockings, and breeches, which were to be wrapped in red taffeta. The First Gentleman of the Bedchamber would then assist the king into the right sleeve of his nightshirt, and the First Gentleman of the Wardrobe into the left, and so on.

How could thousands of the most powerful members of the nobility be kept at court during a lifetime of such tedious procedures? Endless entertainments were devised to ease the boredom. Versailles functioned very much like a grand resort hotel. The vast gardens seemed to reshape all nature. There was a good deal of hunting during the day and a good deal of card playing at night. The most brilliant intellectuals were encouraged to stay at court, and conversation was delightful. Versailles was a sort of paradise. According to *The Larousse Encyclopedia of Modern History:*

> The flower beds were renewed twice a day by means of interchangeable pots. Hundreds of wax torches, supported by masked figures, turned night into day, illuminating the foliage as brightly as the sun. Tropical plants bloomed in the depths of winter. Invisible musicians lured the wanderer toward labyrinths and fountains. At nightfall, on some enchanted isle, theatrical spectacles and ballets would take place under a shimmering canopy of fireworks. In these spectacles, the King himself would play a leading role: the simple shepherd, the conquering hero, or perhaps Jupiter among the gods.

And so the nobility of France were prisoners of their own pleasure. How could life in an uncomfortable provincial estate be compared to this?

Courtiers who displeased the king and were banished from court frequently committed suicide.

As at a grand hotel, fashion in dress was all important. The king set the style, and the style he set was one of the most elaborate in the entire history of dress (Plate 1). Louis was quite short, and boots were replaced by silk stockings and high-heeled shoes of silk and velvet, encrusted with gems. Men wore thick brocades heavy with gold and silver embroidery. One outfit might be decorated with three hundred bows. The entire effect was surmounted by a huge wig of heavy curls falling on the shoulders, of a style adopted by the king when his hair became thin. In the words of Madame de Sévigné, one of the most brilliant women of the court, such an outfit might cost "the eyes out of your head." Women's dress was equally sumptuous. Moreover, French styles were carried to the farthest corners of Europe by means of dolls dressed in the latest fashion, which were sent from Paris regularly to broadcast the latest rage. An aristocrat, neglecting his estates while at court, might easily impoverish himself in keeping up with the fashions as etiquette required. This was just what the king intended.

While the nobility played, Louis was busily at work. He replaced the aristocrats throughout the provinces with his own representatives, who ruled in his name, forming a huge bureaucracy. He established new industries and assisted those that existed. He reorganized the army and gave it a new code of honor. And all power was centered in his hands. Ruling by "divine right," he could say with a clear conscience, *"L'état, c'est moi,"* ("I am the State"). He saw himself as the sun, whose rays make all life possible; he was the Sun King.

We can imagine that Louis's court would be a great center for all the arts, and so it was. The Renaissance love of classical art had come to France in the seventeenth century, as it had come to Spain, in the form of the Baroque. But in France (and this was not true in Spain) there was a tremendous taste for everything pertaining to ancient Greece and Rome. Racine (1639–1699) wrote his great tragedies modeled on the Roman, and the gods of Olympus sport in the bitingly witty satires of Molière (1622–1673). In fact, no artists have painted modern man's notions of classical tranquillity as did the two greatest French painters of the seventeenth century, Nicolas Poussin (1594–1665) and Claude Lorrain (1660–1682).

Botticelli and the artists of the Italian Renaissance painted classical subjects in a Renaissance setting, but in the seventeenth century such play of time and location was no longer possible. Men had a clear idea of the way the world looked in their own century and how it looked two thousand years before, and they were determined to escape into, to re-create in living flesh, an ideal world they felt must have been inhabited by the ideal statues of classical times (Plate 2). Poussin and Lorrain painted as if remembering some golden age before their own soiled and torn era — one of a peaceful tranquillity that the unadorned lines of classical architecture suggest, but that never was (Plate 3).

Classical art was of course pleasing to Louis with his passion for order, and he set about remodeling the visual world as he remolded the society that inhabited it. In the seventeenth century most of the visual world was still medieval. Stone buildings had not been torn down, and many churches and castles of the Middle Ages still stood. Renaissance architecture had only just come to France. In the towns, narrow streets were overhung by half-timbered houses; there was little light and no sanitation. Thatched cottages dotted the countryside. Louis wanted to clear away this medieval world to make way for broad avenues and allées of trees, wide courtyards, vast Baroque palaces, and endless gardens. At Versailles, troupes of artists were kept busy creating sculptural stucco and gilded decorations and executing vast wall paintings celebrating the godlike greatness of the king, while hundreds of statues were commissioned to adorn the gardens. All this activity was carefully organized. Much of the work at Versailles was directed by the king's official painter, Charles Lebrun (1619–1690), a leading figure of the French Academy, which formulated strict rules to control all the arts — literature as well as sculpture and painting. But of course, final decisions lay with the king.

In the seventeenth century the power of the king grew out of all bounds in France, but in England it was given a deathblow. Charles I had very much the same idea of the strength of the monarchy as did Louis

2. Nicolas Poussin. *Apollo and Daphne*, about 1665. *Paris, Louvre.*

3. Claude Lorrain. *The Embarkation of the Queen of Sheba*, 1648. *London, National Gallery.*

XIV. But the staunchly Protestant middle class of England, most especially the Puritan sects, had too strong a sense of the traditional English liberties to accept his notion of his position. Parliament challenged the king's power, and the result was civil war. The Parliamentary "Roundheads," led by Oliver Cromwell, actually defeated the king and had him put to death.

Eventually the people, tired of republican experiments, invited the heir to the throne to return, and restored the monarchy. Still, this exercise in bloodshed was not in vain and from that time on, the kings of England recognized that basic power lay not in the monarchy but in Parliament.

This is not to say that any decisions rested with the people. The nobility, and the wealthier gentry and merchants, many of whom succeeded quickly enough in attaining titles and social position, were in control and went unchecked even by the king. Their way of life, like that of the French court, was an art in itself.

Court life held no interest for the English, and London was their meeting place only for a yearly "season." They preferred the country. Vast estates covered the countryside — often at the expense of the small farmers, who were pushed off the land and driven to seek work in the city. Meanwhile, tenants tilled the soil of the owner, and superb parklands surrounded the "great houses" that varied in size from comfortable manors to rural palaces. The English country gentleman was traditionally not interested in fashion or in art; he was interested in hunting, fishing, and caring for his estates.

Still, the greater nobility owned fine collections of paintings and sculpture. But this was foreign art, never English, Charles I collected Italian masters, knighted Rubens, and employed Rubens's pupil Anthony van Dyck as court painter. Foreign artists were always welcome in England. The Great Style — splendid compositions on religious, mythological, or historical subjects in the manner of the Renaissance masters Michelangelo and Raphael — was much admired, but it does not seem to have entered anyone's mind that an Englishman might be capable of painting such works. One nobleman spoke for all when he said, "You surely would not have me hang up a modern English picture in my house unless it were a portrait."

But portraits there were. Any Englishman with a claim to gentility wanted a portrait of himself and his family, and by the eighteenth century England could boast a group of portrait painters as fine as any in Europe.

Probably the first among these portrait painters was Sir Joshua Reynolds (1723–1792). Reynolds was very much a man of his time — a friend of Samuel Johnson and the political firebrand, Edmund Burke. Reynolds was also the first president of the Royal Academy, established one hundred and twenty years after the founding of the French Academy. On the occasion of the Royal Academy's opening, Reynolds said, "It is indeed difficult to give any other reason why an empire like that of Britain should so long have wanted an ornament [the Academy] so suitable to its greatness, than that slow progression of things, which naturally makes elegance and refinement the last effect of opulence and power." Certainly, few artists in history have been better suited than the English portraitists of the eighteenth century for depicting opulence and power with elegance and refinement.

Reynolds himself admired the "heroick" style of Michelangelo and Raphael and adapted it as often as possible to his paintings. So, in his portrait of the actor David Garrick (Plate 4) he has used the figures of Tragedy and Comedy to give the dramatic effect of a work in the Great Style.

Sir Thomas Gainsborough (1727–1788) won fewer official honors, but enjoyed a long and successful career as a portraitist, with a studio in the fashionable resort of Bath. Gainsborough had less formal training than Reynolds and he never visited Italy. But he loved the English countryside and the fresh faces of English beauties, no matter how lavishly the ladies were dressed, and he combined his loves (Plate 5), placing his women swathed with taffeta and lace into a rural setting. This was as it should be in England, where the most sumptuous wealth was devoted to country living.

There were other artists as well, like George Romney (1734–1802), whose appreciation of the soft pink-and-white complexion of English women made him the perfect master to paint Lady Hamilton (Plate 6), the famous beauty who rose from the station of cook to become the wife of Lord Hamilton and the great love of Lord Nelson.

4. Sir Joshua Reynolds. *Garrick between Tragedy and Comedy*, about 1761. *England, Private Collection.*

Strangely enough, the first artist in England to try his hand successfully at something more than portraiture and landscape painting and to attempt the Great Style was an American, a Pennsylvanian Quaker, Benjamin West (1738–1820). Needless to say, in the British colonies of North America, painting followed the English style. The American portraitists John Singleton Copley (1738–1815) (Plate 7) and the younger Gilbert

5. Sir Thomas Gainsborough. *Mary, Countess Howe*, about 1760.
   London, Kenwood, Iveagh Bequest.

6. George Romney. *Lady Hamilton in a Straw Hat*, about 1785. *San Marino, California, Henry E. Huntingdon Art Gallery.*

Stuart (1755–1828) both settled in London and painted portraits with the gracious ease of a Romney or a Reynolds. The latter, in fact, encouraged Copley to come to England. Stuart's portraits of Washington (Plate

8. Gilbert Stuart. *George Washington* (detail), eighteenth century. *Boston, Museum of Fine Arts.*

7. John Singleton Copley. *Mrs. Thomas Boylston,* 1765. *Cambridge, Massachusetts, Fogg Art Museum.*

8) are known to every schoolchild; surprisingly, there are more of these to be found in England than in the United States.

West, too, settled in England. His painting, *The Death of Wolfe* (Plate

9), the general whose forces defeated those of French General Montcalm on Quebec's Plains of Abraham in 1771, affected the course of European painting. The composition is not very original; it is like many paintings of the Deposition of Christ. But this was the first time that a contemporary event had been painted in contemporary dress (although the picture is not historically accurate). Oddly enough, such scenes were usually lifted out of the present and depicted in a classical setting. (At Versailles, Louis XIV was painted entering Dunkirk in a golden breastplate and grasping a thunderbolt.) West even went so far as to paint medieval subjects in carefully researched medieval costume, and the painting of modern history was born. He eventually became president of the Royal Academy, but as a Quaker he refused to accept the honor of knighthood.

9. Benjamin West. *The Death of Wolfe*, 1771. *Ottawa, Ontario, National Gallery of Canada.*

Portraits of the English gentry and historical paintings alone would give a one-sided view of eighteenth-century England. There was another less agreeable side to English life. Poorer farmers, driven off the land as their wealthy neighbors extended their estates, took refuge in the cities where, for the lucky, work was to be found in the new textile factories and sweat-shops. For the unlucky, there was no work at all and the only livelihood was thievery. The wealthy who set foot out at night were surrounded by servants to protect them from the bands of cutthroats who patrolled the streets. In vain the authorities organized public executions for the smallest offense. These executions became public holidays, and the pockets of the crowds were picked by other offenders, yet uncaught. Meanwhile, whole families lived on a loaf of bread a week, often sharing a tiny room in a filthy back alley.

The world of pickpockets and thieves and the poor and the follies of the rich — all these appealed as subject matter to William Hogarth (1697–1764). The son of a poor schoolmaster, Hogarth was trained as an engraver, but his ambition was to be a painter. In order to support his wife and family he turned to the usual field of portraiture. But he was always at his best painting people of the street. Hogarth was devoted to realism in every detail. He discovered "by mortifying experience, that whoever would succeed in this branch [portraiture], must make divinities of all who sit for him." Unfortunately, there was no market for paintings of the seamier side of London, no matter how lively.

Then, in 1728, Hogarth hit upon a kind of art that suited him and would sell. He found that if he portrayed a series of scenes of low life that told a story in narrative form and sold them cheaply as engravings, he could reach a wide audience. He particularly liked moral tales such as *The Rake's Progress*, the story of a frivolous young man's descent through gambling and debauchery to the madhouse, all depicted in grisly detail. *Marriage à la Mode* tells the story, in various scenes, of the worthless and empty marriage of a fashionable young couple. Scene ii (Plate 10) takes place in the morning. The husband has had too much to drink the night before, the house is a total mess, and the bride can cope with nothing, least of all her accounts. No detail of their shoddy lives — the unused vio-

10. William Hogarth. *Marriage à la Mode*, scene ii, 1743. *London, National Gallery.*

lin, the untrained dog — has escaped the artist's notice. This characteristic is what made his works fascinating — in fact, fun to look at. In Plate 11 we see a scene in Newgate Jail, drawn from John Gay's *The Beggar's Opera* in which the heroes are highwaymen and thieves.

But if the destitution of the poor and the folly of the rich were noticeable in England, in eighteenth-century France they were carried to extremes. For all its magnificence, the reign of Louis XIV ended shabbily. Greed for military glory led Louis into a series of disastrous wars. He saw himself, moreover, as the savior of Catholic Europe and he oppressed and tortured the Protestants, driving some two hundred thousand, many of them well-educated craftsmen, out of France. Foreign trade was cut off, industry ruined, and the country bankrupt. Louis tried desperately to raise funds, but we must remember that the aristocracy, those so amply enter-tained at Versailles at the expense of the state, paid no taxes. Money had to be raised by taxing the *bourgeoisie*, and the peasants, who were already starving. Times were bad and people on the land were driven to eating acorns and bread made of couch grass and ferns. It is hardly surprising that there were uprisings throughout France and that crowds shouted, "Let us do what the English did to their king."

Criticism was in the air. The Catholic Church maintained the divine, God-given right of kings, but now the old beliefs were questioned, and questioned more seriously than ever before. The advance of science and the explorers' discovery of a globe populated by peoples who were not Catholic or even Christian and yet who possessed undeniable wisdom, made doubt and criticism inevitable. John Locke (1632–1704), spokesman for the revolution in England, wrote that government was based not on the will of God but on a kind of contract between the ruler and the gov-erned, and that the people were in fact the sovereign. In France, his ideas were followed by those of Montesquieu (1689–1755). Meanwhile, the royal engineer Vauban recommended tax reforms and better treatment of

11. William Hogarth. *The Beggar's Opera*, about 1731.
    London, Tate Gallery.

the poor, and fell out of favor at court. All hopes were pinned on the new monarch. Unfortunately, these hopes were disappointed.

Louis XIV died in 1715, leaving as his heir his five-year-old grandson. After a period of confusion during the rule of regents in his childhood, the young king announced that he meant to rule for himself. Handsome and charming, Louis XV had good intentions. Unfortunately, he was lazy. He soon tired of government and allowed his favorites at court to do as they pleased. Under Louis XIV, the king had worked while the court-iers played. Now the king joined the fun. With the aid of his mistress, Madame de Pompadour, a woman of excellent taste, the king devoted the rest of his reign to enjoying himself, and that at a time when the most serious problems faced France. But if he was determined to enjoy himself, he did so with an unashamed splendor. Like all ages given over to pleasure, his reign was a great period for the arts.

All the arts of France were admired, imitated, and copied throughout Europe. Just as, in the eighteenth century, the French language was the language of diplomacy, the language spoken in all the courts throughout Europe, so French cuisine, tapestries, furniture, and porcelain set the style from Gibraltar to Moscow. But the heavy, ponderous, and serious designs of the seventeenth century no longer appealed to a French court given over entirely to frivolity. Deliciously curling lines, exquisite delicacy, still more exquisite colors, shades of the palest pinks and blues, mauves and grays — these were what pleased a court in which refinement had gone too far. Madame de Pompadour designed for one of her residences a gar-den made entirely of china flowers so cleverly perfumed that they even deceived the king. This new style was called Rococo.

The first of the Rococo painters was also the greatest, Jean Antoine Watteau (1684–1721). Watteau admired the work of Rubens, but his figures were more delicate, their movements more quiet. One could say, almost, that they floated in a dream. And the subjects Watteau chose were something quite new. He painted, not the personifications of gods and goddesses at play, so popular a century before, but the courtiers them-selves at play: idling, flirting, watching a performance — again, as seen in a dream. *The Embarkation from Cythera*, the island of Venus, Goddess

12. Jean Antoine Watteau. *The Embarkation from Cythera*, 1717. *Paris, Louvre.*

of Love, is one of Watteau's masterpieces (Plate 12). Couples are departing arm in arm, led by a flight of cupids. This picture has often been mistakingly called "The Embarkation for Cythera." In fact, the couples are *leaving* the Island of Love, reluctantly, and the mood of the picture is one of wistful melancholy. There is a note of melancholy in all Watteau's work, perhaps because he had tuberculosis and knew he would die young. He often painted theatrical performers and clowns, lost among the greenery of paradisiacal gardens like those of Versailles. Yet we do not want to laugh at his painting of the clown Gilles (Plate 13). As he stands awkwardly, the ridiculousness of his satin costume makes us rather want to cry. It is this sense of the tragedy under the mask of frivolity — a tragedy all too near and yet not recognized — that made Watteau one of the great painters of the century.

The artists of the following generation imitated Watteau's lovely landscapes and his richly dressed courtiers and players, but they removed the

13. Jean Antoine Watteau. *Gilles*, 1721. *Paris, Louvre*.

element of tragedy and their paintings are particularly empty. The most sucessful artist, François Boucher (1703–1770), was more an admirer of Rubens than of Watteau. Boucher was willing to try his hand at anything — portraits, *genre* scenes, landscapes. But he was best known for his nudes — pink, rosy-cheeked, well turned, and pretty. Boucher was certainly a man of his time, and a favorite of Madame de Pompadour, whom he painted (Plate 14) dressed in the lace, taffetas, frills, and flowers, embroidered and real, that were the Rococo fashion. She commissioned him to paint the walls of her château at Bellevue, the site of the china flowering garden.

The art of Jean Baptiste Siméon Chardin (1699–1779) tells us more of the simpler life of the French: not of the peasants, but of the *bourgeoisie*, the thinking people, whose world was one of neatly kept houses (with

14. François Boucher. *Madame de Pompadour*, about 1757. *Edinburgh, National Gallery of Scotland.*

servants, of course), of familiar household objects — boots, an inkstand, a toy — of women in starched white aprons, and men in russet velvet coats. Chardin was most especially a painter of children — eating, quietly playing games, or going about their studies (Plate 15). Yet so superb was his smooth technique and so touching were his pictures that they were admired by the very same courtiers who patronized Boucher.

Still, neither the well-ordered, homely domestic world of Chardin nor the giddy mindlessness of Boucher was a true mirror of the age, any more than the placid, wise Madonnas of Leonardo were of theirs. There were ugly problems and violent answers. A group of thinkers, the *Philosophes*, many of them educated members of the middle class, were joined by aristocrats who could see all too clearly the faults of the society in which they lived. By now, most of the aristocracy had moved back to apartments in Paris, and certain hostesses were known for entertaining the intellectuals of their day. These women were clever, often attractive, and brilliant at drawing out conversation, and at their salons — regular, informal gatherings of groups of friends — talk went unhampered. Thinking had become fashionable and it ran along lines that would have shocked an earlier generation. The *Philosophes* not only attacked the Church; some were admitted atheists. Both Church and State felt the barbs of Voltaire (1694–1778), the most witty and brilliant of all, who churned out essays, tragedies, satirical tales, and endless letters, attacking injustice wherever he found it. Diderot, d'Alembert, and others produced the *Encyclopédie*, an encyclopedia of all human knowledge as seen through the eyes of the Enlightenment. The Swiss Jean Jacques Rousseau (1712–1778) wrote that all society was based on a social contract and that man was most happy in a state of uncontracted nature.

What action did the king take against attacks on the monarchy? Voltaire was exiled and the works of the *Encyclopédiantes* were banned, but efforts at punishment were halfhearted. Too many members of the state understood and approved the ideas of the Philosophes. But the king himself, Louis XV's grandson, Louis XVI, did not understand. He was not an unkind man — not unkind enough even to try to stamp out criticism. But on the other hand, neither was he wise enough nor strong enough to make the necessary reforms. His wife, the Austrian Marie Antoinette, was, if anything, even more foolish and blindly extravagant. The majority of the aristocracy refused flatly to give up their privileges.

Meanwhile, the French court continued to see the world through a bower of posies. Boucher's successor, Jean Honoré Fragonard (1732–1806), continued to paint scenes of delicate coquetry. He was a more interesting painter than Boucher, and his landscapes have a solemn beauty (Plate 16). But he was not more serious than Boucher. In 1766 he painted *The Swing* (Plate 17). Ten years later, a group of men in Philadelphia declared that "all men are created equal."

15. Jean Baptiste Siméon Chardin. *The Young Schoolmistress*, eighteenth century. *London, National Gallery*.

16. Jean Honoré Fragonard. *The Big Cypresses of the Villa d'Este*, about 1760. *Besancon, France, Musée des Beaux Arts.*

17. Jean Honoré Fragonard. *The Swing*, about 1766. *London, Wallace Collection.*

In 1789 the blow fell. France was bankrupt, prices were inflated, and the crops had failed. There was famine in the countryside and starvation in the cities. Above all, there was a clamor for reform. Louis XVI was forced to call the Estates-General, the French Parliament, which had not met for one hundred and fifty years. It was divided into three Estates — the Clergy, the Nobility, and the Third Estate, the mass of the common people. When the Third Estate broke away and declared itself the legislature of France, all authority crumbled. The throngs from the back streets of Paris formed a mob, terrifying and unpredictable. It attacked and tore down the Bastille, the hated, although rarely used, royal prison. In the countryside, bands of brigands looted the great châteaux. A hysterical mob of the women of Paris, shouting for bread, marched on Versailles. The king invited them to take whatever the royal bakeries could provide, but they wanted "the baker" (the king) himself. And so the royal family was taken prisoner and marched back to Paris.

The revolution came in relentless wave after relentless wave with each new group of "reformers" putting to death, in a kind of madness, those who had preceded them. The only solution for disagreement seemed to be death. One by one they all went to the guillotine, the newly invented machine for painless decapitation. Everyone who had had anything whatever to do with the old order, the *ancien régime* — the king, the queen, the aristocrats who would not have reform, the aristocrats who passionately wanted reform, the pastry chef in the kitchens at Versailles, and the reformers themselves — all alike waited with hair cut short at the nape of the neck for the blade to fall. The Rococo world was beheaded.

VI
The
NINETEENTH CENTURY

MUCH LIKE OTHER MEN in other eras, those who shaped the new world of the nineteenth century wanted it to be different, not only socially and politically but also visually. The new French Republic was to be the Roman Republic restored to life. As if changing their role by changing their costume, the women who had worn mountainous powdered wigs, who had pinched their tiny waists, and who had swept about in the wide and bulky skirts of the "old order," the *ancien regime*, now dressed like Roman matrons in narrow classical garments, high-waisted and simply draped. They wore their hair its natural color, tied in a knot at the back like that of a Greek statue. The revolutionaries called themselves the *sans culottes*, which meant literally that they were without knee breeches. This item of clothing disappeared, too. The opening of the nineteenth century found men sensibly dressed in trousers reaching the ankle, while jackets and waistcoats took a more modified form, and fussy laces disappeared almost completely. In theory, the revolution put an end to extravagant wealth — to all extravagance, with one exception. As we shall see, there was still a good deal of extravagant sentiment.

Kings and courtiers at play no longer provided a subject for artists. The sterner legends of Rome were more in keeping with the spirit of an age that had seen so much bloodshed in the name of Reason, Morality, and Justice. *The Oath of the Horatii* (Plate 1) was not a subject that would have appealed to Fragonard. The Horatii were three Roman brothers who swore to fight three brothers of Rome's enemies, the Abans, in single combat. This canvas was painted by the one man who might have been called the artist of the French Revolution, Jacques Louis David (1748–1825).

David was the son of a haberdasher and a relative of the painter Boucher. In 1775, David went to study in Rome and there he developed his Neoclassical (literally "new" classical) style. Although the art of Greece and Rome had served as a model to Europeans since the Renaissance, it was not until the eighteenth century that serious archaeological excavation began and there arose an altogether new interest in classical art. The cities of Pompeii and Herculaneum, buried since the explosion of Vesuvius in A.D. 79, were slowly unearthed; travelers were actually visiting Greece itself and bringing back sketches of the Parthenon and the great buildings of the Golden Age. The art historian Johann Winckelmann first realized what the Greeks had in fact tried to do — to create, by following the dictates of reason, forms of perfect beauty. He wrote: "To take the ancients for models is the only way to become great, yes, unsurpassable, if we can." And David, the artist of the revolution that took Rome as its model, followed Winckelmann's instructions to the last detail. He even went so far as to put exact replicas of Roman furniture in his compositions.

David threw himself into the revolution. He was a member of the Third Estate in the national assembly; he voted for the death of the king, and he feverishly painted and sketched the historic scenes he helped to create: Marat murdered in his bath and looking like a fallen Roman hero; and the listless Marie Antoinette, haggard and aged, led to the guillotine. Even his paintings of classical subjects, *The Oath of the Horatii, The Death of Socrates,* and *Brutus with His Dead Son,* were meant to inspire

1. Jacques Louis David. *The Oath of the Horatii*, 1784. *Paris, Louvre.*

devotion to the revolution. The Horatii, Brutus, who sentenced his own son to death for treason, and Socrates — all were men who put the good of the state before their private interests. The leaders of the French Revolution were expected to do this to an excessive degree, as one after another they were sentenced to death by their rivals for power. Only when his own hero Robespierre was executed and he himself was imprisoned in the Luxembourg Palace did David begin to question the justice of the revolution.

Meanwhile the Neoclassical style spread throughout Europe, to Germany, Italy, and England. It spread everywhere that the spirit of revolution, the new spirit of liberty and equality was felt, and most especially to America, to the "Roman" republic of the United States. Architecture was particularly influenced by Neoclassical ideas; for this reason, many public buildings of the period in America were designed with the handsome foursquare proportions and the columned porticoes of ancient Greece and Rome. The Capitol itself, at Washington, is such a building. Often Greek or Roman ideas were cleverly adapted to the needs and materials of the country. Apart from his many other talents, Thomas Jefferson was an architect. When he designed the University of Virginia (Plate 2), and his own home, Monticello, he applied the glistening white columns and pediments of Greek architecture against a background of the good red brick of Virginia.

The French Revolution was not as tidy, as well-balanced, as the American Revolution. It was a revolution that ran away with itself, and bloodshed led not to order but to further bloodshed, further confusion. Moreover, the governments of France's neighbors, the monarchies of Prussia and Austria, marched on Paris in a futile attempt to save the monarchy. They were soon joined by virtually the entire remainder of Europe: England, Spain, and Holland. To meet the threat, the National Convention which then ruled France did something never done before: it drafted all men of fighting age into a national conscript army. At home the Reign of Terror eventually gave way to a period of calm, but a true democracy had not taken root. All too clearly, a strong leader was needed, and he was found in the person of a young general from Corsica, Napoleon Bonaparte, who put down the last insurrection in Paris with "a whiff of grapeshot."

In this era of civil strife and disorder the only power within France lay in the huge, newly conscripted army; this army was behind Napoleon, who first made himself director and finally emperor. It must not be thought, though, that France had returned to monarchy. Although ruling with absolute power, Napoleon attempted in his way to preserve the ideals of the revolution, to reform the ancient laws under which France could no longer function — the laws that divided a class of privileged aristocrats

2. Thomas Jefferson. The Rotunda at the University of Virginia, nineteenth century. *Charlottesville, Virginia.*

from the people. Moreover, Napoleon saw that the best way to stifle conflicts at home was to march his great armies across Europe and beyond, defeating the enemies of France and bringing them the reforms of the revolution. All those who were young, who were active, who were discontent in France, followed this indefatigable man to "glory," to victory, and sooner or later to death on battlefields as distant as Egypt and Russia.

If Napoleon brought with him the ideals of the French Revolution, he brought with him, too, the art of the revolution. David was quickly won over and he painted the coronation of Napoleon and his wife, Josephine (Plate 3), almost as if it were the coronation of a Roman emperor, despite the presence of several bishops and the Pope. Napoleon does not wear a crown, but rather, in true antique fashion, a golden wreath of laurel leaves. He saw Europe as "united" in his newly won "Roman" empire, and wherever his victorious armies set foot, columns and porticoes sprang up to flank façades; Roman reds and purples replaced the pastel shades of the eighteenth century; and the severe Roman lines of what is called the Empire style replaced the delicate curves of the Rococo.

David was not the only neoclassical painter. He was followed by a talented band of students and imitators such as Antoine Jean Gros (1771–

3. Jacques Louis David. *The Coronation of Napoleon and Josephine in Notre Dame* (detail), about 1807. *Paris, Louvre*.

1835), whose huge compositions celebrated the military victories and travels of the emperor. In Gros's painting *The Pesthouse at Jaffa* (Plate 4), the visiting emperor shows no fear of contagion as the inmates regard him with swooning gratitude. Artists of other European countries followed France's lead. The greatest sculptor of the early nineteenth century, the Italian Antonio Canova (1757–1822), portrayed Napoleon's sister Pauline Borghese as a draped nude goddess on a Roman couch (Plate 5).

But the greatest of all David's pupils and the greatest of all Neoclassical painters was Jean Auguste Dominique Ingres (1780–1867). His *The Bather of Valpinçon* (Plate 6) shows us the exquisite elegance and refinement of the best of Neoclassical art. Almost every object in the painting besides the bather herself is white, and there are an infinite number of shades of white, a multitude of contrasting textures. As we have seen, the

4. Antoine Jean Gros. *The Pesthouse at Jaffa*, 1804. *Paris, Louvre.*

5. Antonio Canova. *Pauline Bonaparte Borghese*, about 1808. *Rome, Borghese Gallery*.

Romans translated flesh and blood into cold stone, and that cold stone seems to have found its way into the exquisitely finished paintings of the Neoclassicists with their hard, fine lines and shallow shading.

With the defeat of Napoleon, David followed his hero into exile. When he died in Brussels in 1825, the Neoclassical age was very nearly over. The ideals of the revolution and the empire of Napoleon, which had inspired Neoclassical art, were no more than memories, having little to do with the problems and realities of a new era. But Ingres continued to paint in the cool, serene style of his master for another forty years, throughout the changes and upheavals that made the nineteenth century a narrow, crowded bridge linking all of history to the present.

We have been speaking of the French Revolution, but there had been another kind as well, one that shook the world of the eighteenth century

6. Jean Auguste Dominique Ingres. *The Bather of Valpinçon*, 1808.
   Paris, Louvre.

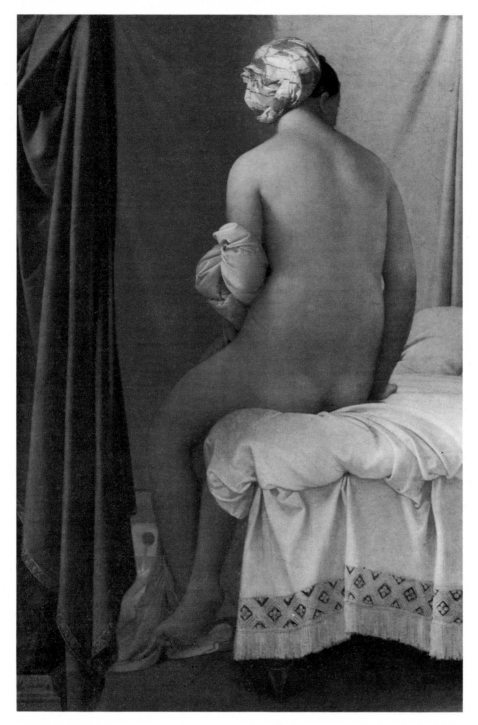

to its foundations — the Industrial Revolution. We have noticed, over the centuries, western man's growing interest in the sciences. In the 1700's this interest blossomed into a series of great inventions: the technique of smelting iron by the use of coal; the flying shuttle, the spinning jenny, and the roller spinning frame, which revolutionized the textile industry; a new process for the production of steel; and most important, the use of steam for power. As one industry after another was converted to the use of steam, mass production became possible and what we call the modern world was born. By the early nineteenth century, one writer remarked, "Two centuries ago not one person in a thousand wore stockings; one century ago, not one person in five hundred wore them; now, not one person in a thousand is without them."

The two revolutions, political and industrial, went hand in hand. All during the eighteenth century there were new opportunities for obtaining wealth. A worker who saved his money might invest in the new industry and make his fortune. And so the growing band of industrialists broke up the *ancien régime* much as the merchants of the towns had destroyed the rigid feudalism of the Middle Ages. When the revolution finally came, most of the poor, despite their marches on Versailles, despite their cheers at the guillotine, remained as poor as ever. But with the class of hereditary privilege removed, there was something new: there was opportunity. Any man, whatever his birth, could rise to wealth and power — there was always the chance; and the new industry made this chance a frequent reality. And so, in the nineteenth-century scramble for wealth, the elements of excitement and hope replaced the more basic reforms envisioned by the revolutionaries.

The chaos created by the two revolutions was accompanied by something new and sinister, a visual ugliness never before seen. The factories themselves were eyesores, built with little or no attention to beauty. They burned coal to create the necessary steam power, and belched black clouds into the air that had been clear since the creation. The coal was dug from mines that were in themselves hideous.

But most important, the conversion of Europe and America from a world of home industry to one of vast factories posed social problems as yet unsolved. Village industries died and the poor in search of work flooded into factory towns where squalid slums sprang up. We must remember that there was no sanitation, no public health, and little city government to cope with such a problem. What had already been a disgrace in the eighteenth century became a monstrous scar on the face of society. The slums were masses of ugly hovels far more offensive to the eye than the age-old rural dwellings of the poor, with their dirt floors and thatched roofs. Children worked long hours in the factories, and family life almost disappeared. The Industrial Revolution had its birth in England, as Europe's political revolution had been born in France, but by the mid-nineteenth century both upheavals were spreading throughout the Continent and bringing their problems with them.

The cool, serene lines of Neoclassical art may have reflected the political ideals of the revolution, but they could not reflect the striving, convulsive turmoil of the nineteenth century. There was a new spirit in the air: the desire of a world that had broken all the restraints of a rigid social order to break all restraints in art and literature as well, the desire to feel things more deeply and to say them more passionately. This new stirring was called Romanticism.

We first see the spirit of Romanticism in the paintings of the Spanish artist Francisco José de Goya y Lucientes (1746–1828). Goya began his career as a successful portraitist and eventually a court painter. He created, with great style, portraits in the eighteenth-century mold, paintings of exquisite silks and jewels and of pale flesh; he might have been working at the court of Louis XVI. But his portrait *The Family of Charles IV* (Plate 7) exhibits an insight that no Boucher or Fragonard ever possessed. The fact is that, although their clothing is exquisite, these are not pretty people. With few exceptions, faces of blank stupidity stare out of the painting. At the very moment he painted this portrait, Goya was undergoing a profound spiritual change. A serious illness had left him deaf, but this change was not due entirely to his own suffering. Goya witnessed the general commotion and upheaval of his time when Napoleon brought war to Spain as he did to the other countries of Europe. The Peninsular War, as the war in Spain and Portugal was called, was particu-

7. Francisco Goya. *The Family of Charles IV*, 1800. *Madrid, Prado.*

larly bloody. Spain was mercilessly used as a battlefield for the contending
forces of Napoleon and the English, whom he wished to cut off from
trade with Portugal; in the course of the conflict Napoleon simply seized
control of both peninsular countries. As all the armies involved lived off
the land, the country was ravaged, farms were plundered, and the innocent were murdered, while disease spread from the troops to the towns.
With the assistance of England, the Spanish and Portuguese banded together to throw out their invader and Napoleon was eventually distracted
by problems elsewhere. Goya observed and portrayed the follies that
seemed sensible to most of Europe but that to him seemed a kind of
madness.

In 1799, Goya had produced a series of etchings called *Los Caprichos*
(*The Caprices*), depicting, as he put it, "the multitude of follies and

blunders common in every civil society." This series was followed by another yet grimmer, *The Disasters of War*. These are not light commentaries, but monstrous visions from deep in the imagination (Plate 8). Under a sinister and leaden sky, atrocities of the most monstrous nature are committed. Corpses hang by the neck; others are dismembered; others are left to lie obscenely about the landscape. Huge birdlike figures descend on mankind. All that is sacred is made to appear grotesque.

The Disasters of War was not seen by the general public, but those who knew Goya asked him why he had turned to such hideousness for his art. His answer was very plain. He wanted "to have the pleasure of saying eternally to men that they should stop being barbarians."

In his last years, Goya decorated the villa to which he retired with his *Pinturas Negras* (*Black Pictures*). In these nightmares of the soul, witches cavort (Plate 9) and cannibals devour human bodies. Figures are no longer carefully painted, but are suggested with a few murky smears of the brush. These paintings are not social comments on the nature of war; they are statements on the natural evil of man. Was Goya mad? He may

8. Francisco Goya. *Bury Them and Be Silent:* from *The Disasters of War*, 1810–1813.

9. Francisco Goya. *Witches' Sabbath*, 1820–1822. *Madrid, Prado.*

well have been. What is most amazing is that his art was tolerated, even applauded, by the very society he depicted so scathingly. Like El Greco's, his genius was appreciated, however far it was from artistic fashion — perhaps because Spain herself was far from the fashionable centers of art. If we compare these works of Goya's with those of his contemporaries Fragonard and David, we can see that Goya's mind is literally in another world. But to the romantics he was an inspiration.

Romanticism, then, had its birth in a kind of divine madness, and in England another tortured soul was painting his inner visions, although these visions were very far from Goya's. William Blake (1757–1827) remained an impoverished engraver all his life. This strange man had mystical experiences of a deeply religious nature. He claimed that he received messages from heaven, and that he had dined with Isaiah and Ezekiel. He translated these visions into poetry, which he illustrated with pictures (for the most part pen-and-ink drawings and watercolors) of strange and ecstatic beauty. His two greatest books were *Songs of Innocence* and *Songs of Experience*. Some of these "songs" are of childlike simplicity, while others are more sinister. Blake believed in social reform. Isaiah had told him, he claimed, that "honest indignation is the voice of God." Blake sympathized with the French Revolution, until the terror turned him away in disgust. Above all, he was one of the first to cry out against the ugliness created by the Industrial Revolution. As with everything, he felt it passionately:

> And did the Countenance Divine
> Shine forth upon our clouded hills?
> And was Jerusalem builded here
> Among these dark Satanic Mills?

The Whirlwind of Lovers (Plate 10) is typical of Blake's sketches — figures wafted in divine grace. The art of Goya and the art of Blake, born deep in what was later called the "subconscious" imagination, was something entirely new. Moreover, it was little appreciated. Blake remained a pauper, and only in his old age did he find a small circle of admirers. But by that time the yearning to break out of the confines of accepted art forms, to express deep and impassioned emotion, had blosomed into its full

10. William Blake. *The Whirlwind of Lovers*, about 1824. *Birmingham, England, City Museum and Art Gallery.*

force. This "romantic" movement was international and it encompassed all the arts. The staid, measured polyphony of Bach was replaced by the grand, sweeping symphonies of Beethoven and the emotional outpourings of Schumann, Schubert, and Chopin. The neat, rhythmic couplets of Pope were replaced by the supernal, impassioned lines of Shelley and Keats. The romantics sought, in the words of Shelley:

> Some world far from ours
> Where music and moonlight and feeling are one.

Byron, dark-eyed and suffering, was the hero who stood apart from society and mocked it. And so the arts, too, had their revolution.

Above all, the romantics sought to escape — escape from the sordidness of industrial Europe with its money grubbing and hopeless slums, escape

11. John Constable. *The Leaping Horse* (study), about 1825. *London, Victoria and Albert Museum.*

from the bonds of any man-made social order. Byron fled as far as Greece, but others were content simply to seek peace in the country.

Now nature was most admired as it began to be destroyed. Although landscape painting dates from the sixteenth century, it now became a vogue. Moreover, the romantic painters wanted truly to return to nature. The Englishman John Constable (1776–1837) was the first artist actually to make a habit of taking his easel outdoors. This may be the reason why his peaceful landscapes, although finished in his studio, were far fresher in color than anything painted before. His foliage was more truly green, his skies more truly blue, and for this he was criticized. Often, in his hurried sketches, such as *The Leaping Horse* (Plate 11), the brushwork is swift and imprecise because he wanted to catch the feel of the moment. For him, painting was "but another word for feeling."

Constable's contemporary Joseph Mallord William Turner (1775–

12. Joseph Mallord William Turner. *The Slave Ship*, 1840. *Boston, Massachusetts, Museum of Fine Arts.*

1851) was a painter of a very different sort, although equally romantic. He bathed his views in a diaphanous atmosphere of radiant light, but these were not always or even often the cozy scenes of his native England. He preferred more dramatic subjects: the Alps emerging from the glittering morning mists or the lagoons of Venice merging with the sky, storms on land and gales at sea. Often one dark, recognizable element formed a focus of attention in his whirling conflagrations of transparent color. Not only was Turner more dramatic in his choice of subjects than Constable, but he was more emotional in the way he portrayed them. For the romantics there was always emotion, and for the landscape painters it was the passionate emotion of nature itself. In the words of Shelley, Turner was in search of: "hues as when some great painter dips his pencil in the gloom of earthquake and eclipse." In Turner's *The Slave Ship* (Plate 12), the sea is alive, driven wild with the fire of the sun. Birds flap their wings; sea and sky form one impassioned atmosphere, and we realize that this is not a picture of sea or sky or a boat, but of an emotion. It may seem very different from Constable's *The Leaping Horse*, but both paintings have this in common: they are landscapes in motion, dramatically composed, and we feel the energy of the artist in every stroke.

Both in Germany and America, Romanticism was expressed most often in landscape painting. Joseph Anton Koch (1768–1839) was born in the Tyrol and all his life painted the stony grandeur and sweeping cataracts of the Alps. A painting such as his *The Schmadribach Fall* (Plate 13) again expresses the romantics' wonder at the drama of nature. And yet

13. Joseph Anton Koch. *The Schmadribach Fall*, 1811. *Leipzig, Germany, Museum of Fine Arts.*

this is a painting of some kind of Olympus, and one feels that no mountain was ever so high or perfectly formed, no fall of water so steep. Like all romantic paintings, it portrays the human striving to exceed all bounds, even those of the beauty of nature itself. The work of Thomas Cole (1801–1848), such as *The Oxbow of the Connecticut* (Plate 14), is scarcely less dramatic. On the left, black clouds pour rain onto a black landscape while to the right are the peace and sun of paradise. It is not surprising that in America, where the grandiose aspects of nature were still best seen, landscape should have interested artists more than figure painting. Thomas Cole himself, although born in England, was taken as

14. Thomas Cole. *The Oxbow of the Connecticut*, 1836. *New York, Metropolitan Museum of Art, Gift of Mrs. Russell Sage, 1908.*

a youth to Ohio, then a frontier, where he taught himself to paint. He eventually settled in the East, on the Hudson River, still wildly beautiful as it meandered between its dramatic cliffs. In fact, the Hudson River gave its name to an entire school of landscape painters, most of whom lived on its banks, which have a certain mysterious romance about them to this very day. Some of those artists, like Frederick Edwin Church (1826–1900), traveled as far as the Arctic, the tropics, and the Near East for inspiration, but all of them painted with Cole's sense of drama and of the wonder of nature. For two hundred years, nature had been the settlers' enemy, but now, in the nineteenth century, it could be enjoyed.

Not all the romantics chose escape into nature. Others chose escape to faraway lands or to the depths of the past. This is not surprising; during the nineteenth century, archaeology grew as a science, and the map of the world was finally filled in as explorers charted previously unknown regions of Africa and Asia. Moreover, the period of political revolution in nineteenth-century Europe was accompanied by a vast growth in learning and by experiments in free public education. More people could read than ever before and newspapers circulated. In the eighteenth century, Voltaire himself had thought that there was a tribe in central Asia with aprons of flesh on their bellies, but by the mid-nineteenth century the Moslem countries of North Africa and the deserts of Asia were no longer places of fable. They were not yet truly known, however; they piqued the imagination.

Moreover, periods of history other than classical were explored. What had life been like at the court of the Sultan of Turkey in 1600 or in the crusader castles of the twelfth century? Now that horizons had been widened, a European might ask such a question, and the artist might search for images with which to reply. Napoleon's armies returned from Egypt with tales of the tombs of the pharaohs, and within a decade the obelisks and sphinxes had crept into the backgrounds of stylish portraits, and little replicas of them graced fashionable drawing rooms.

Eugène Delacroix (1798–1863) was, in a way, the master of romantic escape. Like Byron, Delacroix was a figure to inspire the romantic imagination. He had tigerlike good looks; he was a dandy; he was rumored to

15. Eugène Delacroix. *The Women of Algiers*, 1834. *Paris, Louvre.*

be a son of the statesman Talleyrand. He drew his subjects from every period of history, from the Bible and mythology. The Arabs and Negroes of North Africa, the life of the harem (Plate 15), and lion hunts particularly fascinated him, and a trip to Morocco in 1832 served as an inspiration for the rest of his life. Even when Delacroix painted the revolutionary uprising of Paris in 1830 (Plate 16), the scene is one of the imagination, and the figure of Liberty herself, a heroic giantess, leads the masses. In

16. Eugène Delacroix. *Liberty Guiding the People*, 1830. *Paris, Louvre.*

these paintings the clear, firm lines of the Neoclassicists have melted into splashes of color and action. Delacroix wrote, "When the tones are right, the lines draw themselves."

In England, where the need to escape was strongest, the escape was most deliberate and most complete. While the French romantic soul sought the exotic fascinations of the Orient, the English, consciously or unconsciously, chose to flee into the Middle Ages, the period of the past so different from the industrial present. Heroines true to the highest ideals of Victorian womanhood clambered through the plots of novels set in the period of the Crusades, and false Gothic ruins were built all over England while an imitation of Gothic architecture, with an impressive somberness all its own, replaced the Neoclassic.

At the center of this "Gothic" revival stood the critic John Ruskin (1819–1900), a man who abhorred the industrialization of England with particular venom and foresaw many of the almost insoluble problems it would create. Ruskin favored a most unusual group of young artists whose work was not like anything yet seen anywhere and who called themselves the Pre-Raphaelites.

The Pre-Raphaelites felt that the true inspiration of art had died with Raphael. His work, they claimed, and that of the artists who had succeeded him throughout Europe, was hollow and empty of true feeling. Since the early Renaissance, artists had not been painting from nature, but rather had been imitating each other. The Pre-Raphaelites, seeking their inspiration in the past, painted subjects from mythology, the Bible, literature, and most especially the Middle Ages, but their desire to look at the world afresh led them to a peculiar kind of realism. So we are aware that when John Everett Millais (1829–1896) painted *Ophelia* (Plate 17), he was not copying some often repeated cliché image of what Ophelia should look like, but was painting the corpse of a real girl, water-sodden and very dead. The result is perfectly dramatic, and in a way perfectly horrifying. Dante Gabriel Rossetti (1828–1882), who was also, like Blake, a poet of first rank, produced an *Annunciation* (Plate 18) that is far from a repeti-

17. Sir John Everett Millais. *Ophelia*, 1852. *London, Tate Gallery.*

18. Dante Gabriel Rossetti. *The Annunciation, 1850. London, Tate Gallery.*

19. Albert Pinkham Ryder. *The Temple of the Mind, before 1888. Buffalo, New York, Albright Knox Art Gallery.*

tion of the overly sweet imitations of the Madonnas of Raphael, so long popular. In Rossetti's painting we see a strange, introspective girl, a girl of the nineteenth century, confused and frightened, rearing back from the news she has received. The canvas has the fresh color of daylight, and the setting is one of symbolic white, a touch of romantic drama.

Among the romantics there were those artists who withdrew not toward nature or other periods in human history but, like Goya and Blake, into their own minds. One of the most interesting of these was the American Albert Pinkham Ryder (1847–1917). Like Blake, Ryder was little known or appreciated during his own lifetime. Although he almost never left his small New York apartment, he painted landscapes and seascapes — but not of the usual kind. In a setting of night, these are landscapes of the mind, visions that the artist dreamed, that we too have dreamed, and that we recognize (Plate 19). They come from the unconscious, the world that the new science of psychology was just beginning to disclose.

Not all the artists of the nineteenth century turned and fled in romantic desperation from reality. Others took a hard look at the world around them, found it touching and even inspiring, and felt that they had something to say about it. Some even tried to improve it. Gustave Flaubert (1821–1880) wrote his pitiless portrait of the French provincial middle class, *Madame Bovary*, and Honoré de Balzac (1799–1850) and Émile Zola (1840–1902) examined French life from top to bottom with a humanity perhaps never equaled in prose. In England, Charles Dickens (1812–1870) described the seamy side of life among the poor and became one of the most widely read authors in any language. Meanwhile, many artists revolted against the artificiality of Neoclassic art not in a romantic desire to express more violent emotions but in a desire to portray man's daily life as they actually saw it, stripped of all affectation — something never really done before.

Oddly enough, Goya, the first of the romantics, was also the first of the realists. We have said that his scenes of war were "romantic" because they were full of passion and drama and even horror. But they are horrible because they are starkly real. If we compare them with Delacroix's *Mas-*

sacre at Chios, we can see immediately that Goya had a message that Delacroix's romanticism would never have delivered.

We have not spoken of French landscape painting in the nineteenth century because the greatest French landscapists of the period were realists, not romantics. They were groups of painters who went to live in the little town of Barbizon, not very far from Paris. Visiting Barbizon today, one might wonder exactly why an artist should choose it as his home. The countryside is flat, with small hillocks, fields, and patches of forest. There is nothing dramatic about the scenery, nothing breathtaking about the views. But the artists of Barbizon were seeking the usual — not the unusual — the homey, the beauty that is to be found in the familiar. The painting of Théodore Rousseau (1812–1867) entitled *Spring* (Plate 20) has nothing of the romantic about it at all. If we quickly compare it with the scenes of Joseph Anton Koch or Thomas Cole, we can see in a moment the difference between the romantics and the realists. Yet Rousseau's gentle, flat landscape appeals much more to the senses than do the

20. Théodore Rousseau. *Spring*, 1852. *Paris, Louvre.*

splendid romantic compositions with their soaring heights and great depths. We feel that we can almost smell the fresh greenery; we know immediately from the formation of the clouds that it has just rained; and we can tell that the grass will be wet. We know that as we come near the pond our feet will sink into the mud on the bank.

Jean Baptiste Camille Corot (1796–1875) was perhaps the most famous of the Barbizon painters, although he did not live in the village and was a constant traveler, whose kinship with the "school" at Barbizon was only spiritual. During his long career, Corot developed a style easily recognizable as his own. He often painted leafy landscapes of deep foliage illuminated by a silvery light (Plate 21), like those scenes one sees at evening when colors are dimmed or like the effects of photography, which was just at that moment first being put to use.

But Corot was also a figure painter, and his *Woman in Blue* (Plate 22) is painted exactly as she would have looked if we had come on her unaware in some poorly lighted nineteenth-century drawing room or studio.

21. Jean Baptiste Camille Corot. *A Leaning Tree by the Water's Edge,* nineteenth century. *Rheims, France, Musée des Beaux-Arts.*

22. Jean Baptiste Camille Corot. *Woman in Blue*, 1874. *Paris, Louvre.*

Nothing has been improved by art. She does not have the luscious, rosy flesh favored by painters from Raphael to Delacroix. Her skin is sallow — a little flabby, but not exaggeratedly so. It is not ugly; it is simply the flesh of a woman who is no longer eighteen. She leans heavily on her elbow; her hair is not in place — strands have escaped from the bun. Her dress is of quite ordinary material. It is not the gorgeous silk that so often appealed to painters of the past, even to Goya when he was being most ruthlessly real. Everything about the figure is humdrum, everyday, and yet for that very reason it is all the more touching.

But Corot was primarily a landscape painter. It was his friend Gustave Courbet (1819–1877) who gave "realism" a name and a deliberate direction. Courbet was an active reformer, deeply involved with the problems of poverty and social injustice. He was a friend of the reformer philosopher Pierre Joseph Proudhon, who felt that painting must reflect man's social environment, and who wrote, "Painting . . . can only consist of the representation of real and existing things." Courbet, who claimed to have no master, painted "real and existing things" in his own robust style. In his *Portrait of the Artist with a Black Dog* (Plate 23) Courbet, practically dressed in a checked wool suit, has obviously been out for a walk. He sets aside his cane, puts down his book, and sits on the rocky ledge of a hillside. Genre paintings of everyday life had existed before, as we have seen, but Courbet's works were totally uninfluenced by ideas of what was graceful or ideally charming. They were far closer to unposed photographic reality. Velázquez had attempted this, but his subject matter was the life of princes and even his beggars found themselves in the company of gods. Moreover, such pictures were usually small, decorative pieces. Courbet's paintings were large. Life-sized figures in everyday clothes strode through his canvases, annoying or shocking the public. When Courbet painted workingmen, as in his *The Stone Breakers* (Plate 24), there was nothing charming or decorative about them. There was straining, sweat, torn and dirty clothes, and no drama. Such visions did not please the public. When his work was rejected by the Paris Exposition in 1855, Courbet opened his own exhibition entitled "Realism, G. Courbet."

As was the case with David before him, Courbet's involvement in poli-

23. Gustave Courbet. *Portrait of the Artist with a Black Dog*, 1842. *Paris, Musée du Petit-Palais.*

24. Gustave Courbet. *The Stone Breakers*, about 1850. *Winterthur, Switzerland, Collection of Oscar Reinhart.*

tics led to dire results. During the Franco-Prussian War the socialist commune seized power in Paris and named Courbet the president of artists. As a result, he played a role in the removal of the Vendôme Column, a symbol of Napoleonic grandeur. When the commune fell, Courbet was charged with the column's destruction and was imprisoned. Upon his release he fled to Switzerland where he eventually died, like David, in senseless exile.

When Courbet painted a workingman he was a true laborer, but Courbet's message was the heroism of life as it was. He painted everything — beautiful women, nudes, animals, landscapes, even intellectuals chatting or peering at the artist painting a model in his studio. Some other artists struck more directly at social problems, challenging the viewer to think, and think clearly, about the lives of the poor. Among these artists were Jean François Millet (1814–1875) and Honoré Daumier (1808–1879).

Millet, unlike Courbet, was one of the Barbizon painters. He painted, however, not the landscape, but the human figures who inhabited it — the French peasants. Millet himself was of peasant origin, but as a young man he devoted himself to imitations of Fragonard and Watteau. It was not until he was in his thirties that he began to paint the peasant life he had known as a child, and painted it with such conviction, such a solid reality, that he was immediately successful. These figures were not the jolly peasants of Brueghel, or the delicately pretty shepherds and shepherdesses of Boucher; they were men and women whose clothes were rumpled and drenched in sweat, whose heavy clogs sank into the earth. When they heaved a saw (Plate 25) it was not with ease but with great effort. Millet was not a colorist; he painted in lights and shadows. Effort is portrayed in the strong outlines of the woodcutter's leg. Millet managed to give to his peasants the strength and nobility of gods without even making ideal human beings of them. When they stop work to pray at the tolling of the Angelus (Plate 26) they represent the labor of all mankind and ennoble it.

It was the life of the harried city dweller that inspired Daumier, who had lived in Paris from early childhood. He saw life first as an office boy, then as a clerk. By the time he became a lithographer and cartoonist (he was never in the truest sense a painter), he knew the frustrations, the

25. Jean François Millet. *The Woodcutters*, nineteenth century. *London, Victoria and Albert Museum.*

26. Jean François Millet. *The Angelus*, 1859. *Paris, Louvre.*

heartbreak, the humor, and the chicanery of the people of Paris through and through, knew them with his *eyes*. As a political cartoonist and satirist, he was frequently in trouble. The clever, powerful line of his pen lampooned every foible of society — the corrupt judge (Plate 27), the dishonest shopkeeper. He even caricatured the king, Louis Philippe himself, and landed in jail. But with that same pen line he captured the timeless strength of the working people resting their bulky forms on the hard seats and breathing the fetid air of *The Third Class Carriage* (Plate 28). Like Millet, Daumier had a message: the men and women who labor, the toilers, are the true nobles, on whose backs society rests and depends — and this at a time when the international labor movement was first formed and workingmen were demanding better conditions and a fairer share of the growing prosperity. Millet and Daumier were among those who posed the labor question; the answers were to determine the history of the next hundred years.

27. Honoré Daumier. *Grand Stairway in the Palais de Justice*, nineteenth century. *Baltimore, Maryland, Musem of Art*.

28. Honoré Daumier. *The Third Class Carriage*, nineteenth century. *New York, Metropolitan Museum*.

1. Édouard Manet. *Le Déjeuner*, 1868. *Munich, Germany, Neue Pinakothek.*

VII

The MODERN WORLD

ODDLY ENOUGH, it was the search for greater realism — visual realism — that led to a step in the history of art that was a great jump, a leap into what we call the modern world.

A group of painters, all somewhat younger than Courbet, felt that light had never been properly portrayed on canvas. All kinds of light interested them — the brilliant, eye-searing light of the sun or the shimmering, uncertain light of a lamp. They noticed that the eye did not actually see the sharp outlines that painters had used to convey reality since the time of the cave artists. What the eye saw was blotches of color, and these merged to form shapes — shapes that, in very brilliant light or in flickering, dimmed light or at a great distance, became diffused. Shadows, they realized, are not seen as darker shades of the color of the object as we know it to be, but as different colors, as light is reflected and its reflections multiplied throughout the visual world.

Perhaps the first artist to experiment seriously with light was Édouard

Manet (1832–1883). Manet was a realist who admired Courbet, and it was as a realist that he suffered. His prosaic everyday figures, like the boy leaning on a table in *Le Déjeuner* (*The Lunch*) (Plate 1), outraged the public by their matter-of-factness, their lack of "art." But there is something unusual about the treatment of the subject as well. The color is flat. It lacks the usual lustrous finish. The boy's trousers, the tablecloth, the glasses and dishes on the table, the figure of the serving maid behind, the light on the vase next to her — all, at close examination, are seen to be a mosaic of splashes of color that do not blend into one another by degrees, but rather, contrast with one another. It is only one short step from this picture to Manet's *The Bar at the Folies Bergères* (Plate 2). Here the scene is almost entirely reflected; the artist has used the device of a mirror behind the barmaid, who stands ready to take an order. The world that we see is a mass of blotches of splashing color — dark on light, light on dark. Nothing is clearly seen, but we know that a mass of people are present, illuminated by great flickering orbs of gaslight and massive chandeliers. It would be hard to identify a specific figure, but perhaps no artist before had given such an alive, such an immediate, sense of a crowd. These two paintings are fourteen years apart, and in the interim Impressionism was born.

The father of true Impressionism was Manet's close friend Claude Monet (1840–1926), the son of a Parisian grocer. As a young boy, Monet grew up in Le Havre, where the artist Eugène Boudin first persuaded him to paint landscapes in the open air. This experience was a revelation to Monet, who from that time forward struggled with the problems of presenting the light of day. At nineteen, he went to Paris and fell immediately under the spell of Delacroix, Courbet, and the Barbizon painters. His style was always at odds with what was accepted and when he went to study at the studio of the renowned teacher Charles Gleyre, he and a group of friends set themselves apart from the other students. In 1836, the little group spent Easter together, painting in the forest of Fontainebleau. Apart from Monet, the group included Frédéric Bazille (1841–1871); Pierre Auguste Renoir (1841–1919), the son of a Parisian tailor and apprenticed at thirteen in a porcelain factory; and Alfred Sisley (1839–1899), an Englishman born in Paris.

2. Édouard Manet. *The Bar at the Folies Bergères*, 1882. *London, Courtauld Institute Galleries.*

In 1865, Monet enjoyed a small success; two of his views of the Seine were hung in the official Salon of that year. His name was often confused with that of Manet, who now became aware of the young man, who had admired his style for many years. But Monet's success was short-lived. His huge *Women in the Garden* (Plate 3), a truly revolutionary work, was rejected by the Salon of 1867. The picture was so large that Monet was obliged to sink it in a trench so that he could paint the top. Here, for the first time in all art, a canvas actually gives off the light of true sunshine. It filters through the trees, it alights with all its burning brightness on dresses and flowers, the shade itself is warmed, and the beholder squints as if he were standing on the dusty little path, just within the shadows. The entire scene is created by tiny strokes and splashes of brilliant pure color.

In 1870, Monet, fleeing the Franco-Prussian War in which his friend Bazille was killed, went to live in London. There he painted his canvas entitled *Impression: Sunrise* (Plate 4). This time the light was not the sunlight of noon, but the eerie light of a sunrise filtered through the fog and reflected on the oily waters of the Thames. Again, splashes and ripples of color that make no sense when seen at close range create a visual reality

3. Claude Monet. *Women in the Garden*, 1867.
   Paris, Musée de l'Impressionnisme.

true to the way the eye observes. It is no surprise that this picture was painted in London. We can see in a moment which artist had inspired Monet; it was Turner, who beyond all other earlier painters had struggled to put intangible light on canvas.

Once back in France, Monet and his friends became increasingly discouraged by their constant rejection from the Salons, the official gov-

4. Claude Monet. *Impression: Sunrise*, 1872. *Paris, Musée Marmottan.*

5. Camille Pissarro. *Orchard in Flower, Pontoise*, 1877. *Paris, Musée de l'Impressionnisme.*

6. Pierre Auguste Renoir. *La Grenouillère*, 1868. *Winterthur, Switzerland, Collection of Oskar Reinhard.*

7. Claude Monet. *La Grenouillère*, 1869.
   New York, Metropolitan Museum.

ernment-sponsored exhibitions that were so important in French art circles. In 1874 the group organized its own exhibition and was joined by Camille Pissarro (1830–1903), a Portuguese of Jewish descent from the island of Saint Thomas in the West Indies; Edgar Degas (1834–1917); and a well-off young man from Aix-en-Provence, Paul Cézanne (1839–1906). The public reacted to the exhibition with a series of catcalls. Because Monet's painting of the Thames seemed typical of all the work, *Impression: Sunrise* gave rise to the name with which the critics tagged the entire movement. The artists were called impressionists, and the term was not meant to be flattering.

Pissarro was essentially a landscape painter. The young Pissarro was a friend and admirer of Corot and it is not very difficult to see the influence of the older master in the gnarled tree trunks and shimmering effects of his *Orchard in Flower* (Plate 5), painted in the village of Pontoise, which was near Paris and where he eventually settled. Again, as with *Women in the Garden*, we can sense the heavy, balmy air and the warm, moist sunshine as never before in art.

It was Auguste Renoir who filled his impressionist paintings with human figures. In the summer of 1868 he and Monet painted together at the bathing and boating establishment of La Grenouillère. If we compare their pictures (Plates 6 and 7), we can see that their styles at that moment were very much alike. Both had captured, with carefully placed dabs of color, the extraordinary effect of faintly rippling water. No artist had ever succeeded in painting the reflecting surface of water quite so accurately. But Renoir was not content merely to suggest human figures. He was most famous for his nudes (Plate 8). He discovered that the impressionist technique allowed him to capture the many tones of the human

8. Pierre Auguste Renoir. *Bather Drying Herself*, about 1910. *São Paulo, Brazil, Museum and Art Gallery*.

body with a soft appeal that made him the rival of Rubens, whom he greatly admired. Perhaps because he painted the human figure or because he especially loved and portrayed the beauty of women and children, Renoir was in his modest way more successful with the public than were the other impressionists. But he did not find that the impressionist technique always suited his purpose. Later in his career he came to the conclusion that a harder outline was needed to give his figures a more solid presence, and he broke away from the pure Impressionism of Monet.

Degas faced the same problem. This curious man was half American, the son of a wealthy banker. Degas never married. In his later years he was a recluse — fussy, irritable, a hypochondriac who worried constantly about his health. Photography fascinated him, not for its exact reproduction of the visual world, but for the unusual compositions it caught within the frame of a snapshot. Degas worked in pastel as well as in oil to capture the often lively scenes from the side of Parisian life that attracted him — the ballet, the circus, the cafés, and the music halls (Plate 9). He loved to paint women, especially the chance, momentarily exposed views — as if seen through a keyhole — of women washing or perhaps combing their hair. All were caught with the free, hatching lines of his impressionism. But Degas was interested in matters that the other impressionists avoided. He tried to capture motion — the action of a dancer, or the speed of a running horse when he painted scenes of the races, as he often did (Plate 10). The feet of a horse, he reasoned, flash before the eye more quickly

9. Edgar Degas. *The Orchestra of the Paris Opera*, about 1869. *Paris, Musée de l'Impressionnisme.*

10. Edgar Degas. *False Start*, about 1871. *New York, Collection of Mr. and Mrs. John Hay Whitney.*

than they can be seen. Thus, to give a sense of motion, one must paint the moment's "impression" upon the eye. As with light, one must capture the fleeting vision, seen not with an anatomist's knowledge of what is there but with the impressionist's understanding of what is momentarily glimpsed while the human mind fills in the details.

Degas brought something else to his art. If we look at his painting *The Absinthe Drinker* (Plate 11), we will see that he is concerned not only with a technique for presenting visual reality but also with human understanding and compassion. In fact, in this painting, as in many of his works, he has discarded the impressionist's technique as too diffuse. He is not trying to paint a moment's impression of a scene, but rather a tragic state of being — of being disillusioned, frustrated, lost — and this state is eternal. And so, like Daumier, he has enclosed his subject within the powerful embrace of clear, sharply defined lines.

Both Degas and Renoir found that in portraying humanity the brilliant but fleeting effects of the impressionists were not sufficient. Moreover, the younger generation of painters who followed the impressionists rebelled against the limitations of their technique and sought for new ways to express themselves. But, what was most important, the impressionists, in attempting to portray light, had ceased to paint the visual world as it literally was. They had broken with factual reality and this was a break many artists no longer felt it necessary to mend. Since the invention of photography, anyone in possession of a particular kind of small black box could record the details of any given scene. And so the artists of the generation following the impressionists sought a deeper reality, each in his own way.

Paul Cézanne (1839–1906), for example, although he was of the impressionists' generation, felt that their works lacked solidity. Their bright strokes permitted no sense of the essential form of each object. All of nature, Cézanne felt, was modeled upon geometric forms, and these were lost in the mad rush of the impressionists' color. When Cézanne painted a landscape, he wanted to capture the impressionists' sense of atmosphere, but he wanted to do so without losing the solid sense of soil, of rock, of distant water. The son of a well-to-do banker, but crabbed and unsociable,

11. Edgar Degas. *The Absinthe Drinker*, 1876. Paris, Musée de
l'Impressionnisme.

12. Paul Cézanne. *L'Estaque*, about 1883. *São Paulo, Brazil, Museum and Art Gallery.*

he set up his easel in the south of France and painted scenes like his view of L'Estaque, near Marseilles (Plate 12). Cézanne has indeed succeeded in doing what he set out to do. He has kept to the impressionists' technique, but by closely observing the color tone of every tiny surface of the complex view, he has not lost the effect of a solid hillside, although he has achieved a feeling of warm light and of objects seen at a distance.

Cézanne was not only a landscapist. He applied his technique to all objects. In his many still lifes (Plate 13) he attempted to give this same solidity to a jug, to pieces of fruit, or to a table. He seems to have forgotten the rules of perspective, but perspective did not interest him. He sought the inner solidity of things, the patterns they formed before the

13. Paul Cézanne. *Still Life with a Basket*, about 1890. *Paris, Musée de l'Impressionnisme.*

eye, a certain satisfaction that perhaps one might never get from the visual world at all.

For Vincent van Gogh (1853–1890), Impressionism lacked emotional power. Van Gogh, the son of a Dutch minister, bore the sufferings of humanity on his back in the manner of a medieval saint. Probably no artist in history, except possibly Rembrandt, has felt the anguish of poverty and human destitution so deeply. The one question he asked over and over again was, "How can I be of use in the world?" The answer did not come easily. He tried to assist as a lay preacher in an impoverished mining district and failed so completely that he was sent away. He longed for a wife and family, but failed completely to win the affection of a woman or even to keep his friends. In his late twenties he turned to art as an outlet for his yearnings, and here too he seemed to have failed.

The works of the impressionists, with very few exceptions, were lovely decorations. The impressionists were renegades; they turned away from society, which did not accept their art, and their paintings held no social message. When van Gogh painted *The Potato Eaters* (for which we see a study in Plate 14), he turned back to Millet for inspiration. The people in this study are as much of the earth as the food they eat. Their crude, blunt features suggest that they are hardly capable of thought. Their life is of a cold, dark bleakness, and what little warmth we sense in the picture comes from the most humble of things, a plate of potatoes. This, van Gogh seems to be saying, is the human lot. Look at these beings, but do not forget them.

14. Vincent van Gogh. Study for *The Potato Eaters*, 1885. *Otterlo, Holland, Rijksmuseum Kröller-Müller.*

In 1886, on a trip to Paris to visit his brother and most faithful friend, Theo, van Gogh saw at first hand the art of the impressionists. He immediately changed his technique, and his colors became far brighter and clearer. He found that the free brushstrokes of the impressionists could portray more than merely the quality of light. They could be used to express agitation, passion, the deepest emotions. In his painting *Interior of a Restaurant* (Plate 15), one of those cheap, cheerful places that artists frequented, the scene becomes, suddenly, not cheerful at all. It is full of alert, sensitive, nervous life created by intense, jerking brushstrokes.

Meanwhile, poverty and complete lack of recognition dogged the life of the young artist. In 1888 he moved to Arles in Provence for his health, and there the brilliant heat of the sun drove him into a frenzy. He put this heat on his canvases with ever more excited strokes as he painted the dry,

15. Vincent van Gogh. *Interior of a Restaurant*, 1887. *Otterlo, Holland, Rijksmuseum Kröller-Müller.*

crackling fields of the south, often in brilliant yellows, greens, and blues, his brush so thick with paint that it left great globules on the canvas. In his painting of his bedroom in Arles (Plate 16), we can see that exaggeration has taken over to the point of distortion. The floor seems to sway and move, the bed is elongated, and pictures on the wall hover at an angle as if about to crash down into a precipice. This is a simple, bare room with a bed, two chairs, and a table, and yet it gives us an impression of total hysteria. Van Gogh, in fact, was going mad. A few months later, he cut off his own ear in a fit of remorse, and eventually entered an asylum. Within two years he shot himself. He wrote, "There may be a great fire in our soul and no one ever comes to warm himself at it, and the passers-by see only a little bit of smoke coming through the chimney and pass on their way."

Paul Gauguin (1848–1903) was a young stockbroker with a wife and a large family. He dabbled in art. He was interested in the impressionists, bought their paintings, and exhibited his own paintings at their shows. Then in 1883, at the age of thirty-four, his view of life underwent an unusual change. He gave up his job in order to devote his time to painting, and shortly thereafter he gave up his wife and family as well. The rest of his story is one of excruciating suffering and devotion to an art that went almost totally unappreciated by all except a few of his fellow artists.

Gauguin's fortunes plummeted almost immediately and he was forced to take work as a bill poster. But in 1886, the year van Gogh first came to Paris, Gauguin went to the little town of Port-Aven in Brittany. There, in that starkly primitive province where wooden clogs resounded on the dusty paths, where crudely sculpted crucifixes marked the crossroads, and faith was simple, Gauguin and a young friend, Émile Bernard (1868–1941), developed an altogether new approach to art. Gauguin discarded the technique of Impressionism to paint areas of brilliant, flat color marked by strong outlines. He discarded, too, any attempt to paint the visual world in a naturalistic way. His pictures had no perspective, no shadow. He wanted to paint objects, scenes, situations that "symbolized" human emotions, whatever they might be — love, fear, hate, spiritual exaltation. He wanted his pictures to speak directly to the heart and if it was neces-

16. Vincent van Gogh. *The Artist's Bedroom at Arles*, 1888. *Chicago, Illinois, Art Institute, Helen Birch Bartlett Memorial Collection.*

sary to exaggerate a color or a shape in order to do this, then the color or the shape must be exaggerated. Gauguin asked a follower, "How does that tree look to you? Very green? Well, then, use green — the finest green on your palette. And that shadow is rather blue? Do not be afraid to paint it as blue as possible." When he painted *The Vision after the Sermon* (Plate 17), he was depicting a scene from the spiritual, not the actual, life of the Breton peasants. A group of women in their stiff white coifs stand suddenly enrapt by the vision of Jacob wrestling with the angel. The scene is painted in flat surfaces of color that create an immediately arresting pattern, and the vision is seen against a background of brilliant red that burns into the soul of the viewer just as the stained-glass windows of medieval churches bring scenes from the Bible to burning life.

Gauguin's new approach to art, called Symbolism, brought him a group of admiring young followers in Paris, but little general acceptance. In 1891, disgusted with Europe and convinced that its fate was sealed, he sailed for Tahiti.

Gauguin had always yearned for the tropics, and once in Tahiti he settled down to live among the native people. As with the peasants of Brittany, he preferred a simple life, one in which faith is more direct. Moreover, he found in the magical mythology of the Tahitians a rich symbolism he could put to use in his art. Their handsome, solid bodies and languid motions, too, suited his art.

Paintings like Gauguin's last great work, *Where Do We Come From? What Are We? Where Are We Going?* (Plate 18) are pervaded by a

17. Paul Gauguin. *The Vision after the Sermon — Jacob Wrestling with the Angel*, 1888. *Edinburgh, National Gallery of Scotland.*

18. Paul Gauguin. *Where Do We Come From? What Are We? Where Are We Going?* 1897. *Boston, Massachusetts, Museum of Fine Arts.*

sense of mystery. Figures converse meaningfully, but we cannot hear them. A bird, hovering, a statue of a Buddha, cats, an old lady who grieves — all are symbols. But of what? Like all symbols, their origin is in the unconscious mind and they are universal. Gauguin has translated them into flat patterns of color that fascinate us, that have an appeal which is also universal.

Since we first spoke of the impressionists, we have mentioned again and again the artists' poverty and lack of acceptance. This was especially true of the impressionists, and of the artists like Cézanne, van Gogh, Gauguin, and their followers who rebelled against the impressionists and are often called the post-impressionists. The suffering of many of these men was almost beyond endurance. Monet was so impoverished he tried to commit suicide; Pissarro was forced to paint blinds for a living. Starvation may have driven van Gogh to insanity; and in his last years, with no hope of selling his paintings, Gauguin found it impossible to eke out a living, even in the South Pacific. One night he decided to end his life by taking a jar of arsenic into the jungle and consuming it. But this attempt at suicide was a failure.

If these artists survived at all, it was because they helped each other. They were a kind of fraternity. They exhibited together — little of their work was ever exhibited at the official Salons — and they met at the Café Grebois and other scruffy little taverns around Paris to discuss their work. Those who had a little money or a private income helped those who had nothing. Renoir stole food from his mother to feed Monet's starving family. Gauguin, when he was a young stockbroker, bought the works of the impressionists, and Degas bought Gauguin's later paintings. Van Gogh even went so far as to invite Gauguin to share his little house in Arles, although that experiment in working together was a total failure. Many were assisted by Durand-Ruel, one of the few dealers who appreciated their work.

Meanwhile, the public jeered and so did the critics. It was the American painter James Abbott McNeill Whistler (1834–1903) who tried to bring Impressionism to England. The reaction of the critic John Ruskin, who was so fond of the photographic realism of the Pre-Raphaelites, can be imagined. "I have never expected to hear a coxcomb ask 200 guineas for flinging a pot of paint in the public's face," said Ruskin, and the result was one of the most talked-of lawsuits of the century. Whistler won, but the public at large really did think that a pot of paint was being flung in its face.

In the past, individual artists of great talent had lived and died unappreciated. Rembrandt found few buyers in his old age; Blake was never known to the general public at all. But that a whole movement in art should be either despised by the public or unknown to it, that whole schools of artists should paint only for each other and a few well-chosen admirers — this was something totally new, never before seen in the entire history of art. The fact was that the artist had become detached from society.

Why should this be? There were, in fact, two very important reasons. The first was the invention of photography. For the first time, the artist was no longer needed to record the exact details of the world around him. This could be done more easily and more cheaply by the photographer. The portraitist might capture the soul of a sitter, but for the average family this was a luxury; a snapshot would do. Secondly, the democratic states of Europe and America had less need for official art. Individuals such as Louis XIV or Napoleon might well want their personalities and achievements glorified at public expense. However, the elected officials of democratic France of the Third Republic, of England, where parliament was now in full control and the queen little more than a figurehead, and of the United States, had neither the time nor the public funds to "squander" on art. True, there had been other moments in history when the state took very little interest in art — the seventeenth century in Protestant Holland, for example. But the subjects to which the Dutch turned at that time — portraits, street scenes, and the like — were the very sort of familiar subject that the photographer could make available to a wide audience. The artist was now obliged to turn elsewhere for his material, to turn in upon himself, to try to capture visual light or the agonies of the soul or the truth of universally pondered mysteries, as no photographer could. And what the artist produced was not something immediately recognizable, palatable, or even understandable to the public at large.

And so the role of the artist had changed. During the Middle Ages and the early Renaissance he had been a simple craftsman. Later he was a courtier. Now he was an outcast. Moreover, he was a special kind of outcast, a "Bohemian." Henri Murger had written his *Scènes de la Vie de Bohème* (*Scenes from Bohemian Life*), a romanticized account of the lives and struggles of young artists and writers who lived in the cheap quarters of Paris's Left Bank, and his stories were used as the basis of Giacomo Puccini's popular opera *La Bohème*. And so the starving artist in his garret, his fingers numb with cold, became a stock character and gave the public the idea that this was the way an artist should live. For Monet with his starving children, for van Gogh suffering from desperate malnutrition, and for Gauguin, who had scarcely the strength to paint his last great work on the cheapest burlap, it was not so amusing.

Artists had never before been so totally out of step with society. Much of the late nineteenth-century's notion of elegance was founded on the homey taste of Queen Victoria. The Victorians and their equivalents in America, France, and the rest of Europe surrounded themselves with a stifling clutter of overstuffed and elaborate furniture, gewgaws, bric-a-brac, and mahogany and oak paneling, seen through the gloom of a narrow-windowed darkness. The paintings of a Gauguin would have seemed grotesque on the Victorians' walls. Not that these people did not have their favorite artists. They favored the meticulously realistic animal paintings of the successful woman artist Rosa Bonheur, for example. Anecdotes, and sentimental ones at that, were in fashion. The imagination and genius of the romantics had gone out of this kind of art, but it was a while before people realized this.

Meanwhile, as the artists of the new freedom were exploring life and the mind on their own, the Victorian world went on its way, pampered with fans, pillows, and teacups, tightly confined within stays and manners scarcely believable only a few generations later. But the two divergent paths were meeting imperceptibly. For one thing, the new art was winning a wider and wider audience.

This new audience was due partly to a new style in the decorative, the minor arts of furniture, glass, and china design, interior décor, and even

19. Jan Toorop. *The Three Brides*, 1893. Otterlo, Holland, Rijksmuseum Kröller-Müller.

architecture. This style was called Art Nouveau, literally "new art." Art Nouveau favored the flowing, sinuously curling line of long, wavy hair or of the lily stem. In many ways it was a style descended from the tastes of the Pre-Raphaelites. Art Nouveau inspired everything from wallpaper to printed books, and it was adopted with great success by certain serious artists such as Aubrey Beardsley (1872–1898) and the Dutchman Jan Toorop (1858–1928), who were responsible for many superb book illustrations. Toorop's *The Three Brides* (Plate 19) is a masterpiece of the kind of Art Nouveau flourishes that were associated in some vague way with a rather fashionable idea of evil. Art Nouveau was all very strange, very delicious — and the public loved it.

But what is perhaps most important is that Art Nouveau designs became fashionable for interior decoration. Not only did Art Nouveau objects and furnishings take the place of the stuffy trappings of Victorian interiors, but Art Nouveau designers insisted that their interiors be swept clean of the overstuffed and overcrowded hodgepodge that had clogged rooms for a century. They wanted light, air, and space. And so the stage was set for the new art.

The great international fair of the turn of the century was the Paris Exposition of 1900, and it was a tribute to Art Nouveau. Its symbol, the Eiffel Tower, is itself one stupendous Art Nouveau curve of steel into the air, a statement of the future of mechanical power and "clean lines." Moreover, an entire pavilion was devoted to the work of France's greatest sculptor, Auguste Rodin (1840–1917), a genius with the technical skills of a Michelangelo, who was also the man who brought Impressionism to sculpture.

Rodin possessed a technique, a talent for representation so brilliant that the public was forced to take his experiments seriously, and Rodin attempted Impressionism. His *A Man Walking* (Plate 20) is such an experiment. What do our eyes see when we perceive a man walking? We know that one foot is off the ground while his weight rests on the other, but can the eye grasp this quick shift of weight or do we in fact see both feet on the ground? Is this the impression that falls on our sight? The torso of the figure seems unfinished; it, too, is treated with an impressionistic vagueness. We are not really looking at it; we are looking at the figure's legs.

Rodin's experiments were not popular, and some of his works were even hacked up by vandals. But, in 1900, visitors to the Exposition from all over the world, after they had sampled superb food, taken a crosscontinental ride on a miniature Trans-Siberian railway, and wandered through the exotic pavilions of dozens of countries from Africa to Polynesia, could take a trip into the artistic future and view the sculptures of Rodin. The reaction was cautious. When, in 1913, a full array of what was called "modern" art was exhibited to Americans at the Armory Show in New York, the public was so outraged that some of the paintings had to be protected by guards.

And yet the world was heading, at breakneck speed, for a tremendous

20. Auguste Rodin. *A Man Walking*, 1877–1900. *Paris, Musée Rodin.*

change, an upheaval almost without precedent in history. Beneath the surface the change had been constant. Well outside the padded Victorian drawing room, the steamship had replaced the sailing ship, and the world was becoming enmeshed in a network of railway tracks. New forms of construction had been discovered and in America buildings were reaching for the sky. The automobile and the airplane were invented. But, most important, the old social structure was changing from within. More people had more money to spend, a new middle class was swelling the ranks of the old middle class, while labor unions were formed to secure for the worker a fair share of the profit. The whisper of equality had become a shout.

By 1914, Europe was seething with stresses. There were strikes in every Western country, and a newly industrialized Germany was looking to her neighbors for a place to grow. To this day, historians do not agree on the underlying causes for World War I, but on June 28, 1914, an Austrian archduke was shot and shortly thereafter France, England, Germany, Austria, and the United States became embroiled in a fight of unimaginable ferocity. Why World War I was fought with such venom is still not understood, but the bloodshed was appalling. Fifty thousand men might be killed on a single day, and whole generations were lost. The safe, secure world of the nineteenth century was actually annihilated in the conflagration, and a new world was born — a new world that was far freer in every way than anything that had gone before.

The new world of the twenties was socially free. The rigid structure of society that had been left as a kind of skeleton after the French Revolution lay finally in a brittle heap. Now a man of any class could be "self-made" in a few years; it was not a matter of generations before he and his descendants would be accepted. All behavior was freer. Men spoke more freely; women painted their lips, smoked in public, and danced with men cheek to cheek. Freudian psychology had burst upon the world, the secrets of the subconscious were explored, and the facts of sex were no longer mentioned only in a whisper. People actually felt more free physically. Women took down their stiffly pinned hair and then cut it off. Skirts were shortened to the knee for the first time in two thousand years. Men's suits were looser and trousers were so wide they flapped in the breeze. These changes may seem trivial, but they were important because they made the world look different.

There was a new architecture, an architecture of huge windows, open spaces, and long, smooth, "clean" lines, pioneered by the American Frank Lloyd Wright (1869–1959). Automobiles became fashionable and highways ribboned the countryside. People were free to move.

All this freedom had been foreshadowed by the artists who, fifty years before, had broken all restraints and daringly splashed their canvases with pure color. Now a new generation of their followers had grown up and matured and their art was not only accepted by a freer-thinking world, but welcomed by it. People wanted to live in the future, not the past.

The art that had been produced in the last two decades of the nineteenth century and the first two decades of the twentieth century could at last be appreciated and enjoyed. There was a vast, almost unimaginably diverse variety. Little noticed by the general public, this had been one of the great ages of artistic invention. All the younger artists were influenced by van Gogh, Gauguin, and Cézanne — some by one, some by another, and some by all three.

The art of putting pure emotion on canvas, the Expressionism of van Gogh, as it came to be called, was the inspiration for such younger artists as the Norwegian Edvard Munch (1863–1944). His painting entitled *The Cry* (Plate 21) is literally a scream in visual form. At the turn of the century, several young painters who rebelled against the social injustice and stuffy ideals of Victorian Germany formed a group called *Die Brücke* (The Bridge), a sort of commune or guild of artists working together. Finding their inspiration in van Gogh and Munch, they tried to express their impassioned rebellion and yearning for artistic freedom in paintings such as *Wildly Dancing Children* (Plate 22) by Emil Nolde (1867–1956), and what was later called German Expressionism was born. These artists wanted to express the savage in civilized life, not through the primitive emotion of some exotic country, but through the ancient traditions of the north. With the German Expressionists the new modern art had left the confines of France and become international.

The symbolism of Gauguin inspired a group of painters called the

21. Edvard Munch. *The Cry*, 1893. *Oslo, Norway, Munch-Museet.*

22. Emil Nolde. *Wildly Dancing Children*, 1909. *Kiel, Germany, Kunsthalle.*

Nabis (the Hebrew word *nabhi* means "prophet"). Like Gauguin, they interpreted the world in patterns of brilliant color. The most famous of the Nabis, two artists who shared a studio, Pierre Bonnard (1867–1947) and Édouard Vuillard (1868–1940), did not paint views of the exotic Pacific like Gauguin's, but rather brought his technique home, using it to give a vivid excitement and an unexpected beauty to household scenes like Vulliard's *The Flowered Robe* (Plate 23).

In 1905, a group of artists led by Henri Matisse (1869–1954) exhibited a series of paintings so shocking in their free use of color and line that the artists were immediately branded the *Fauves*, meaning literally the "Wild

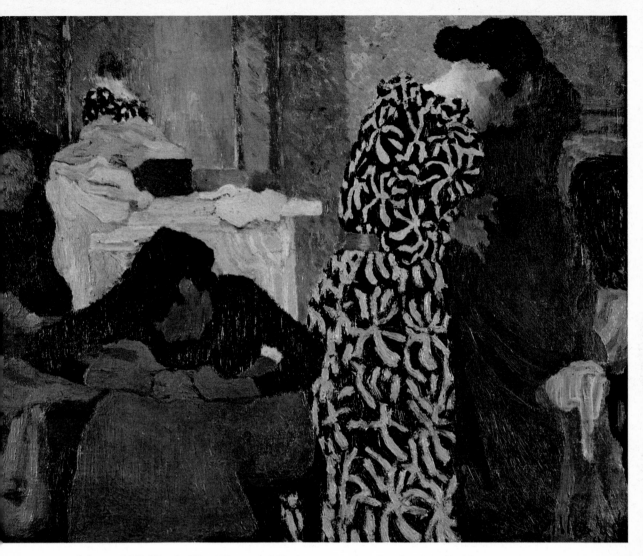

23. Édouard Vuillard. *The Flowered Robe*, 1891. *São Paulo, Brazil, Museum and Art Gallery.*

Beasts." Matisse carried the principles of Gauguin one step further. Gauguin had said that if a tree appeared green, it should be painted very, very green. Matisse felt that if he wanted to paint a nude man blue, he would paint him blue whether he appeared that way or not. In his painting *The Dance* (Plate 24), all sense of accurate anatomy is discarded. The painting is a free expression of the essence of the dance. The figures do not move on legs that are literally believable, but they move with the energy of movement itself. And when Matisse painted a room, it became a flat design representing a room. And yet such a room, like his *Interior at Nice* (Plate 25), gives us an overpowering sense of place, of the sea

24. Henri Matisse. *The Dance*, 1910. *Leningrad, U.S.S.R., Hermitage.*

outside, of the air filled with the late afternoon sun.

Meanwhile, the lessons of Cézanne, as interpreted by two young geniuses, Pablo Picasso (born 1881) and Georges Braque (1882–1963), led to another revolution in art. The son of a Spanish art teacher, the young Picasso first came to Paris to see the Exposition of 1900, but he soon settled at Montmartre and became the hub of a group of young artists, poets, and intellectuals, bohemians like the artists of an older generation, although more carefree — short of cash always, but not starving; not fully appreciated, but not without admirers.

Picasso's early paintings were studies of a touching, humane realism. He used color "expressionistically," so that during his early Blue Period

25. Henri Matisse. *Interior at Nice*, 1921. *Chicago, Illinois, Art Institute, Gift of Mrs. Gilbert W. Chapman.*

color emphasized the hopelessness of beggars and emaciated figures like those who share *The Frugal Repast* (Plate 26).

In his later Rose Period, Picasso turned to acrobats and circus performers for a poignant sense of life and human relationships. But no artist in history has been less content with one style than Picasso. By 1906 he was under the influence of the harsh, simple, and primitive qualities of Spanish Gothic art, and this, added to an enthusiasm for African sculpture, led him to paint *Les Demoiselles d'Avignon* (Plate 27), in which figures are broken down into a totally flat pattern in two-dimensional space. Then, in 1907, Picasso saw a memorial exhibition of the work of Cézanne, who had recently died. Cézanne had been so obsessed with the representation of exact surfaces that, in works like his *Mont Saint-Victoire* (Plate 28), painted just before his death, the entire scene is broken into its component surface areas. The effects of this kind of approach on Picasso were immediate. The already flat objects in his paintings became fragmented. In this way, many angles, many aspects, might be seen at once. The results were such paintings as Picasso's *Violin* (Plate 29). Working hand in hand with Picasso was his friend Georges Braque, a young artist trained as a decorator, who had worked as a Fauve. Braque's paintings (Plate 30), like Picasso's, were accused of being a confusion of little "cubes." These were the words of no less a master than Matisse himself, and so Cubism was born. As Braque put it, the painters felt that by means of fragmentation they could "get closer to objects within the limits that painting would allow" and "establish space and movement in space." The two artists played with their new technique as with a new toy. They were endlessly experimental. Because they were working on flat surfaces, they pasted bits of wallpaper and newspaper into their compositions and so invented the technique later known as collage.

Other artists took up the new Cubism and attempted to give it qualities it did not yet have. A work by Marcel Duchamp (1887–1968), *Nude Descending a Staircase* (Plate 31), for example, attempts to capture the effect of motion in cubistic terms, showing successive views of a moving figure. This painting caused more of an uproar than any other at the 1913 Armory Show in New York. Theodore Roosevelt said that it looked like

28. Paul Cézanne. *Mont Saint-Victoire*, about 1906. *Philadelphia, Pennsylvania, Museum of Art, Collection of George W. Elkins.*

26. Pablo Picasso. *The Frugal Repast, 1904. London, Courtauld Institute Gallery.*

27. Pablo Picasso. *Les Demoiselles d'Avignon, 1907. New York, Museum of Modern Art, Lillie P. Bliss Bequest.*

29. Pablo Picasso. *Violin, 1913. Bern, Switzerland, Kunstmuseum, Hermann and Margrit Rupf Foundation.*

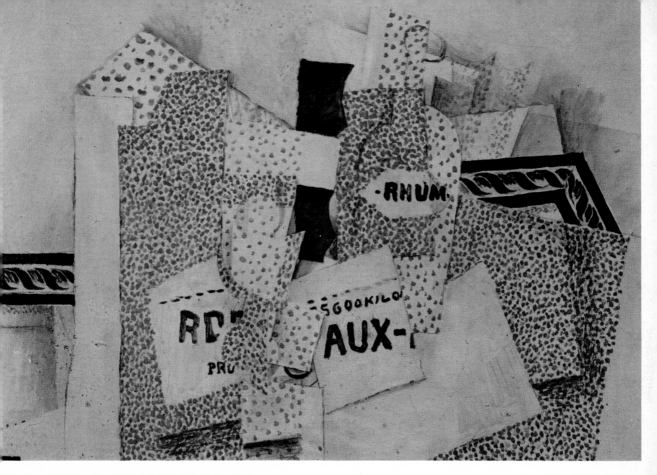

30. Georges Braque. *Bottle of Rum*, 1914. *Garches, France, Private Collection.*

31. Marcel Duchamp. *Nude Descending a Staircase, No. 2*, 1912. *Philadelphia, Pennsylvania, Museum of Art.*

32. Robert Delaunay. *Windows*, 1912. *New York, Solomon R. Guggenheim Museum Collection.*

a Navajo blanket, and a prize was offered to the contestant who could find the nude in the painting.

It was Robert Delaunay (1885–1941) who brought brilliant color to Cubism. To Delaunay, light broke visual objects up into color planes, and these color planes were the true subject for the artist. His painting in

33. Kasimir Malevich. *Eight Red Rectangles*, after 1914. *Amsterdam, Stedelijk Museum.*

Plate 32 is entitled *Windows*, but he felt that nature was "not a subject for description, but a pretext." With that viewpoint, the next step was to drop the "pretext"; the result was totally "abstract" art, like *Eight Red Rectangles* (Plate 33) by Kasimir Malevich (1878–1935), which has no "subject matter" whatever other than itself. In the words of Braque, "Ab-

34. Umberto Boccioni. *Unique Forms of Continuity in Space*, 1913. *New York, Museum of Modern Art, Lillie P. Bliss Bequest.*

stract art is dominated by the same desire for complete freedom and perfection which inspires saints, heroes, and madmen."

And so innovation followed innovation during the teens of the century, and final, complete freedom in art was won at the very moment that the old system finally collapsed in the ashes of World War I. The abstraction of visual forms in art spread to sculpture, and the figures of Umberto Boccioni (1882–1916) in *Unique Forms of Continuity in Space* (Plate 34) suggest movement only roughly based on the striding human figure. Boccioni was a member of a vociferous Italian group called the Futurists. Italians, they felt, and said in a series of screaming manifestos, would have to forget the past and take their place among the creators of the future; the future, as they envisioned it, was the machine age of giant industry. They especially admired violence and speed: "A roaring motor car which runs like a machine gun is more beautiful than the Winged Victory of Samothrace." Boccioni's *States of Mind I: The Farewells* (Plate 35) leaves

35. Umberto Boccioni. *States of Mind I: The Farewells*, 1911. *New York, Private Collection.*

no doubt that the grime, the grimness, the roar, the flashing, fiery power of the steam engine, and the speed at which it will travel, are impressed deep into the minds of the people who have come to a train station to say good-bye.

But the truest expression of the mechanical age was abstract art itself, and it developed quickly. The Russian Wassily Kandinsky (1866–1944), working independently of the cubists, arrived at the notion of abstract art by a different route. To Kandinsky, a landscape need have no recognizable features. The harmony of shapes and colors the artist presented was one of "inner necessity." Kandinsky was absorbed with the inner mysteries of life and with human emotions. His *Little Pleasures, No. 179* (Plate 36) gives us a sense of just that — it breathes life. It could not be more different from the cold but fascinating excercises of Malevich or the severe *Composition with Yellow* (Plate 37) of the Dutch painter Piet Mondrian (1872–1944), who had simplified the patterns of the visual world to their extreme stark mathematical and logical essences.

By the 1920's these innovations had been made. It remained only for them to be appreciated, understood, and digested. The period was one of tremendous excitement and of vast variety in art. Unbelievably, the elderly Monet was still at work, sitting in his garden, creating with dripping paint and a trembling hand images of his lily pond — masterpieces in which Impressionism becomes almost abstract. Bonnard and Vuillard were still at work, turning the domestic world around them into tapestries of brilliant color and always remembering Gauguin. Braque, recovered from his war injuries, was painting his fragmented compositions, but now with a looser grace, and Matisse was painting his wildly colored dreams, although he was turning to sculpture. Picasso, always experimenting, returned to figurative art, painting monumental figures inspired by classical statuary, and then breaking these down into cubistic components. Sculptors like Constantin Brancusi (1876–1957) had turned to total abstraction (Plate 38), seeking the tactile, the touchable effects of basic shapes and the bold outline of three-dimensional abstract form.

This was an exciting world, one in which thinking people were experimenting with their own lives. The "white" rooms designed by Lady

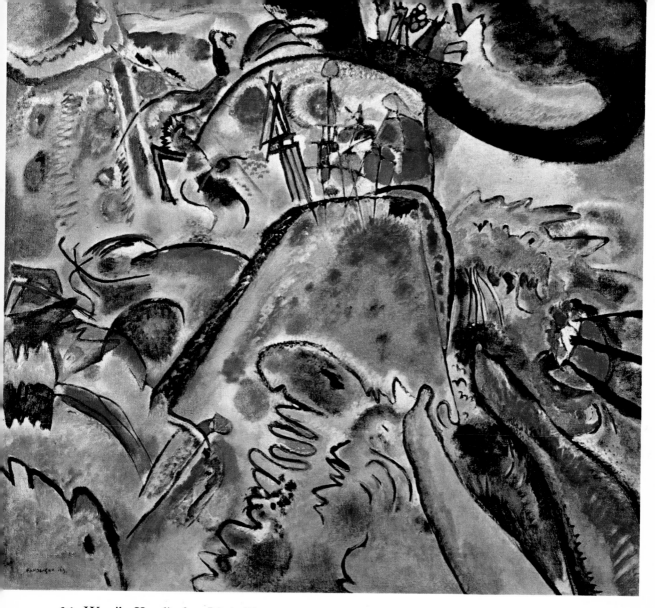

36. Wassily Kandinsky. *Little Pleasures, No. 179, 1913. New York, Solomon R. Guggenheim Museum Collection.*

Mendl; the newly designed and violently simplified "modern" furniture; the airy, smoothly polished experiments of the new architects; all conspired to make a setting for the new, freer art. Modern art was finally accepted in a time of prosperity, when people who enjoyed it could build, design, and experiment.

As ever, new movements and innovations constantly appeared. In 1916, Dadaism came into existence. Dada meant precisely — nothing. Dada

37. Piet Mondrian. *Composition with Yellow*, 1930. *Basel, Switzerland, Collection of Jan Tschichold.*

poets made up verses that meant nothing, using words that meant nothing. The greatest of Dada artists, Marcel Duchamp, exhibited *objets trouvés*, "found objects" such as a public water fountain (Plate 39), or a reproduction of the Mona Lisa on which he had painted a moustache and beard (Plate 40). The Dadaists left one question in the viewer's mind: What is art? The answer has not yet been found.

38. Constantin Brancusi. *Sculpture for the Blind*, 1924. *Philadelphia,
Pennsylvania, Museum of Art.*

40. Marcel Duchamp. *L.H.O.O.Q.*,
1919. *New York, Collection
of Mary Sisler.*

39. Marcel Duchamp. *Fountain*, 1917.
New York, Sidney Janis Gallery.

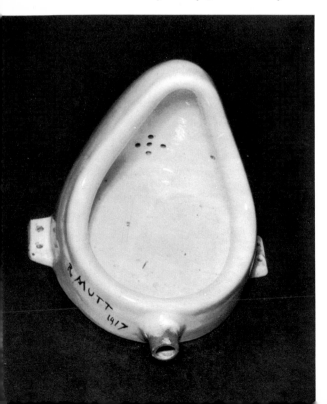

"Thought is born in the mouth" is a statement from the Dada manifesto. It was the habit for groups of young artists working along the same lines to band together, more or less formally, and to produce manifestos stating their aims. Some eight years later, the "surrealists" produced their manifesto, and yet another movement was born. These young artists wanted to give a form to the Dadaists' random "nothing."

André Breton (1896–1966), a literary figure and one of the founders of Surrealism, was a student of Freudian psychology. To the Freudians and the followers of Freud's pupil Jung, dreams were of great importance; they were the key to the thinking of the unconscious mind, where nothing is forgotten, where human frustrations and anxieties work themselves out. The surrealists wanted to put the never-never land of the unconscious, the world of the nightmare or the dream, on their canvases. They wanted to combine dream and reality into a higher "surreality." They admired the strange metaphysical paintings of the Italian Giorgio de' Chirico (born 1888), in which, in a setting of eerie isolation where the eye is carried by perspective lines into the distance, objects from the real world which have no relation to each other lie about at random (Plate 41), giving the viewer the strange sense that he somehow recognizes the scene and is menaced in an inexplicable way. The surrealists realized that dreams are populated with objects and situations that are from the conscious world but are peculiarly juxtaposed in unexpected combinations, as if in a senseless jumble. These are symbols, but symbols of what? According to the psychologist Jung, each mind devises its own symbolism. We can only guess, or else our own subconscious can suggest the answers to our conscious mind. In an etching of a visual poem (Plate 42), by Max Ernst (born 1891), the sinister qualities of a semibarbaric nightmare are almost overwhelming.

Meanwhile, a series of brilliant artists were developing their own very personal styles outside the reach of groups and movements. Nineteen hundred and twenty was the year of the tragic death at thirty-six of Amedeo Modigliani (1884–1920), the young Italian painter who devoted almost all his attention to the human figure, often painting female nudes and portraits. Modigliani concentrated always on recognizable human

41. Giorgio de' Chirico. *The Disquieting Muses*, 1916. *Milan, Italy, Collection of Dr. Gianni Mattioli.*

42. Max Ernst. *Deuxième Poème Visible:* Plate 3 from *Une Semaine de Bonté — Vendredi*, 1934.

43. Amedeo Modigliani. *Nude*, about 1917.
London, Courtauld Institute Gallery.

images. Under the influence of primitive sculpture, which he very much
admired, he carefully molded and elongated his forms (Plate 43) in a way
so personal that it has become synonymous with his name.

The young Russian Marc Chagall (born 1887) not only portrayed
humanity but celebrated it — the poignant humanity that he remembered
from his childhood in the ghetto of Vitebsk, Russia. In his fairy-tale vision,
logic is abandoned and figures float in air, upside down or right side up;
fish carry umbrellas, and donkeys play the violin. Often, some figures are
fragmented in the cubist manner, while others are not. Above all, Chagall's canvases are symphonies of luscious, vivid color. But his colors are
no more logical than his images. The artist's green face looks back into his
past and eye to eye with a sheep in *I and the Village* (Plate 44), a picture
Chagall painted when he first arrived in Paris and was gnawed by home-
sickness.

The giddy prosperity of the twenties did not extend to Germany,
where defeat had brought impoverishment, inflation, and unemployment.

44. Marc Chagall. *I and the Village*, 1911. *New York, Museum of Modern Art, Mrs. Simon Guggenheim Fund.*

Throughout history we have seen art that carried a social message, most notably in the nineteenth century. But in Germany of the twenties and thirties that message was cuttingly sharp, satirical, and terrifying. Artists like Max Beckmann (1884–1950) and George Grosz (1893–1959) observed and chronicled the follies of the rich and the moral decay of their

45. George Grosz. *A Man of Opinion*, 1928. *New York, Collection of Joseph H. Hirshhorn.*

world with a pitiless eye. The rise of Nazism was seen, not as a solution, but as the final, most horrifying degradation. The repulsive Nazi eyeing a bather in Grosz's painting entitled *A Man of Opinion* (Plate 45) was painted in 1928. The artist seems to have a notion of the horror that was in store for the rest of Europe, although it could not yet be foretold.

The thirties were a grim decade. The New York stock market crash in 1929 was followed by a period of economic depression that was worldwide. Meanwhile, the grim powers of Nazism in Germany and Facism in Italy set their icy grip on the arts, dictating what artists and writers were to think and to say and freezing them to a standstill of almost speechless horror. Meanwhile, in France, England, and America, people tried to pay no attention, not to be alarmed. But the middle of the decade was marked by an ugliness, a portent of worse to come. An uprising of the long-abused Spanish populace against their king was mercilessly crushed with the aid of Nazi Germany. Europe looked on, either helpless or undecided about a course of action. Pablo Picasso was one of those who felt the outrage. His huge mural *Guernica* (Plate 46) ranks with Goya's *Disasters of War* as one of the greatest indictments of man's cruelty ever expressed by an artist. Guernica was an ancient Basque town, which was totally destroyed by bombs. Picasso's abstraction is more powerful than any realism could be. A horse whinnies in agony, a dead figure lies dismembered on the ground, a woman looks out into the street and howls, while another woman runs from her house, her body in flames, and a mother cries over her dead baby. A bare electric bulb becomes the blinding flash of a bomb in the night and the entire wall screams. It screams against outrage, and this is the voice of the artist. Picasso wrote, "What do you think an artist is? An imbecile who has only his eyes if he's a painter, or ears if he's a musician, or a lyre at every level of his heart if he's a poet . . . ? On the contrary, he's at the same time a political being. . . . No, painting is not done to decorate apartments." Picasso, like his countryman Goya, wanted "to have the pleasure of saying eternally to men that they should stop being barbarians."

Between 1932 and 1935, Max Beckmann painted a huge tryptich entitled *Departure* (Plate 47). The setting is one of some mythical Nordic past, but the message cannot be mistaken. Men, women, and children are loading ships — fragile, primitive rowing boats. They are already in the water, about to sail. This, Beckmann seems to be saying, is a time when men must flee, must escape a dire menace. With the Nazi persecution of the Jews and anyone who opposed Nazi power in any way, artists and

46. Pablo Picasso. *Guernica*, 1937. *New York, Museum of Modern Art, on extended loan from the artist.*

47. Max Beckmann. *Departure*, 1932–1933. *New York, Museum of Modern Art.*

intellectuals were fleeing, first from one capital of Europe to another, and finally across the water to England and most especially to America. Beckmann himself escaped first to Paris and later to Amsterdam. As the Nazi menace spread like some monstrous plague the list of artists who immigrated to countries that were still free became endless. These men boundlessly enriched the artistic life of the countries where they found refuge. Some stayed behind, like Picasso, who remained holed up in his Paris apartment during the entirety of World War II, flatly daring the devil himself to touch him.

During World War I the horror remained at the front. Behind the lines, life went on as usual despite privations. There was no mass bombing and the Dadaists were free to frame their manifestos of "Nothing" without reference to, or perhaps because of, the bloodshed that was going on not too many miles away.

World War II was very different. In the countries overrun by Nazism, all thought, all creativity, were stifled. Those who did not care to exalt the Nazi or Fascist state were soon enough sent to concentration camps and extinction. Nazi taste in art ran to oversized, muscular, robotlike figures as realistic as dress-shop dummies. The Nazis condemned virtually all of modern art. Even the aged Edvard Munch suffered the disgrace of seeing his paintings, the inspiration of German Expressionism, hung in a Nazi exhibition of "degenerate art."

We can have only the sketchiest notion of how art has reflected history since World War II. It may be many decades before we can step back and achieve some historical perspective. But one definite result of the war and the period preceding it was the development of important art outside continental Europe. In England the painter Francis Bacon (born 1909) carried Expressionism to its most excruciating limits. In Bacon's paintings, figures wince in agony, flesh melts and oozes blood (Plate 48). Bacon portrays not social and political, but personal and psychological, suffering, The art of Bacon is very different from the clear, cool linear abstractions of his compatriot Ben Nicholson (born 1894), as seen in Plate 49. And certainly the figures of Henry Moore (born 1898), gigantic, often abstract, but always human (Plate 50), rank among the most

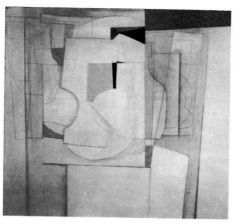

49. Ben Nicholson. *Sept. 14 '53 (Balearic)*, 1953. *London, Gimpel Fils Ltd.* (below).

48. Francis Bacon. *Study after Velázquez' Portrait of Pope Innocent X*, 1953. *New York, Collection of Mr. and Mrs. Carter Burden.*

50. Henry Moore. *Reclining Figure*, 1938. *London, Tate Gallery.*

important in modern art, expressing as they do the monumental solidity, the sense of weight, that has been one of the glories of sculpture from the statues of the pharaohs through the works of Michelangelo to the present.

But it was perhaps the United States that profited most from the influx of European artists. Chagall, Mondrian, Duchamp, Lipchitz, Max Ernst, Dali, and many others had immigrated to America. Before the war, American artists had always felt that a European apprenticeship was necessary. But now they were thrown back upon themselves, and in New York a brilliant group of artists evolved a style known as abstract expressionism.

By looking at their paintings it would be difficult to tell what their works have in common, other than the fact that they are abstract and in most of them some emotion is expressed. The frantically mangled mass of lines and spattered drops of color in the canvases (Plate 51) of Jackson Pollock (1912–1956), the melting squares of color (Plate 52) of Mark Rothko (1903–1970), the angrily slashed-out figures (Plate 53) of Willem de Kooning (born 1904), a Dutchman who came to the United States in his youth, all seem totally different from each other. What, in fact, they have in common is not the way the finished works appear to the viewer, but the actual way in which they were painted. To the abstract expressionists the chance effects of their medium on canvas are all-important. The abstract-expressionist does not try to plan his work, but prefers to let the composition form itself as the artist paints.

It remains only to ask the question, For whom is art produced in the twentieth century? Probably for the first time in history, a great deal of art is created for the enjoyment of the public at large. This is because of the great number of museums to be found everywhere. Museums of art first came into existence in the early nineteenth century; they were a product of the new ideas of the French Revolution. But these museums were largely collections of works from the past, which students could come to study and hopefully copy. Only after the beginning of the twentieth century, when artists and the public in general ceased to look to the past, were contemporary works collected, and museums exhibiting modern art built in the major, and many of the minor, cities of the world.

51. Jackson Pollock. *Full Fathom Five*, 1947. *New York. Museum of Modern Art, Gift of Peggy Guggenheim.*

52. Mark Rothko. *Slate Blue and Brown on Plum*, 1958. *New York Sidney Janis Gallery.*

53. Willem de Kooning. *Woman I*, 1950–1952.
New York, Museum of Modern Art.

This is not to say that private collectors do not exist. They do exist and are important. Now, for the first time, an elaborate international art market has been established, giving works of art a set commercial value. For the first time since the Dark Ages, art is bought for its investment value. the mid-twentieth century, too. Because of advertising, television, and

But the artists have had their say about the commercial nature of life in the growth of magazines and newspapers, a vast number of images pass before us daily, many of them produced for commercial purposes, and our eyes have grown so accustomed to them that we take them for granted. The artists of the movement called Pop Art tell us to stop and look at these images. Like the Campbell's tomato soup can (Plate 54) of Andy Warhol (born 1931), they are often blown up in scale so that we can examine them closely and then ask ourselves what we really think of them. Pop Art, too, reflects a historical change, a questioning of values.

What do we find in art today that tells us most about the society in which we live? There have been a myriad of movements during the last ten years. Apart from Pop Art we have seen Op Art, an experiment in optical illusion; kinetic art, which is to say art that makes use of artificial light or movement; hard edge abstraction with its sharp and precise outlines; environmental art which attempts to envelop us in a total effect; psychedelic art, which reflects the use of drugs in our society; and the new realism, an art so intent on reality that its painting is based on photography and its sculpture on casts of the human body. And this is to name but a few of the movements. It may be that the freedom which we see everywhere in art, this constant experimentation itself, best reflects the complexity of society today — the spirit of questioning and the challenging of long accepted rules and notions which make this an exciting time in which to live.

54. Andy Warhol, *Tomato Soup Can*, 1965. *New York, Museum of Modern Art.*

BOOKS FOR FURTHER READING

Baumann, Hans. *The Caves*. New York: Pantheon, 1964.

Berenson, Bernard. *Italian Painters of the Renaissance*. 2 vols. New York: Phaidon, 1953.

Bibby, Geoffrey. *Four Thousand Years Ago*. New York: Alfred A. Knopf, 1961.

Burckhardt, Jacob. *The Civilization of the Renaissance in Italy*. New York: Phaidon, 1965.

Canaday, John. *Culture Gulch*. New York: Farrar, Straus and Giroux, 1969.

————. *The Lives of the Painters*. New York: Norton, 1969.

————. *Mainstreams of Modern Art*. New York: Simon and Schuster, 1959.

Cellini, Benvenuto. *The Autobiography of Benvenuto Cellini*. New York: Macmillan, 1969.

Chagall, Bela and Marc. *Burning Lights*. New York: Schocken Books, 1946.

Clark, Kenneth, *Leonardo da Vinci: An Account of His Development as an Artist*. New York: Gannon, 1939.

————. *The Nude: A Study in Ideal Form*. Princeton, N.J.: Princeton University Press (Bollingen Series), 1972.

Finley, M. I. *The Ancient Greeks*. New York: Viking, 1963.

Gough, Michael. *The Early Christians*. New York: Praeger, 1961.

Lynes, Russell. *The Artmakers of 19th Century America*. New York: Atheneum, 1970.

Martinelli, G. *The World of Renaissance Florence*. New York: G. P. Putnam's Sons, 1968.

McCarthy, Mary. *The Stones of Florence*. New York: Harcourt Brace Jovanovich, 1959.

————. *Venice Observed*. New York: Harcourt Brace Jovanovich, 1963.

McLanathan, Richard. *The American Tradition in the Arts*. New York: Harcourt Brace Jovanovich, 1969.

Mertz, Barbara. *Red Land, Black Land*. London: Hodder and Stoughton, 1967.

Mertz, Barbara and Richard. *Two Thousand Years in Rome*. New York: Coward McCann, 1968.

Munz, Ludwig. *Rembrandt*. New York: Harry N. Abrams, (rev.) 1967.

Nolthenius, Helene. *In That Dawn*. London: Darton, Longman and Todd, Ltd., 1968.

Oldenbourg, Zoë. *The Crusades*. New York: Pantheon, 1966.

Payne, Robert. *The Christian Centuries*. New York: Norton, 1966.

Protter, Eric. *Painters on Painting*. New York: Grosset and Dunlap Universal Library, 1963.

Rose, Barbara. *American Art since 1900*. New York: Praeger, 1967.

Shattuck, Roger. *The Banquet Years: The Origins of the Avant Garde in France, 1885 to World War I*. New York: Random House, 1968.

Silverberg, Robert. *The Morning of Mankind*. Greenwich, Conn.: New York Graphic Society, 1967.

Sitwell, Sacheverell. *Monks, Nuns, and Monasteries*. New York: Holt, Rinehart and Winston, 1965.

Vasari, Girogi. *Vasari's Lives of the Most Eminent Painters, Sculptors and Architects*. 3 vols. New York: Harry N. Abrams, 1972.

Wyndham Lewis, D. B. *The World of Goya*. New York: Clarkson N. Potter, 1968.

BOOKS SUGGESTED
FOR THEIR ILLUSTRATIONS

Bazin, Germain. *The History of World Sculpture*. Greenwich, Conn.: New York Graphic Society, 1968.

_____. *Twenty Thousand Years of World Painting*. New York: Harry N. Abrams, 1967.

The Book of Art: A Pictorial Encyclopedia of Painting, Drawing and Sculpture. 10 vols. New York: Grolier, 1965.

Seton, Lloyd and others. *World Architecture: An Illustrated History*. London: Paul Hamlyn, 1963.

INDEX

ABOUT THE AUTHOR

Ariane Ruskin was born in New York City and now makes her home there with her husband, the author Michael Batterberry. Together, they have written the ten volume *Discovering Art* series and they are frequent contributors of magazine articles on the arts. Miss Ruskin is the author of *The Pantheon Story of Art*.

Miss Ruskin has worked in publishing and at the United Nations, and has traveled widely in Europe and South America. She attended Barnard College, where she graduated summa cum laude and Phi Beta Kappa. She holds a master's degree from Cambridge University.

133716

DATE DUE
